First World War
and Army of Occupation
War Diary
France, Belgium and Germany

24 DIVISION
Divisional Troops
Royal Army Medical Corps
73 Field Ambulance
21 August 1915 - 30 April 1919

WO95/2202/2

The Naval & Military Press Ltd
www.nmarchive.com
Published in association with The National Archives

Published by

The Naval & Military Press Ltd

Unit 10 Ridgewood Industrial Park,

Uckfield, East Sussex,

TN22 5QE England

Tel: +44 (0) 1825 749494

www.naval-military-press.com

www.nmarchive.com

This diary has been reprinted in facsimile from the original. Any imperfections are inevitably reproduced and the quality may fall short of modern type and cartographic standards.

© Crown Copyright
Images reproduced by permission of The National Archives, London, England, 2015.

Contents

Document type	Place/Title	Date From	Date To
Heading	WO95/2202/2 73 Field Ambulance		
Heading	73rd Field Ambulance Aug 1915-Apl 1919		
Heading	24th Division 73rd Field amb. Vol I Aug to Sept. Dec. 18		
War Diary	Eastbourne	21/08/1915	23/08/1915
War Diary	Bullswater Camp	24/08/1915	01/09/1915
War Diary	Southampton	01/09/1915	01/09/1915
War Diary	Havre	02/09/1915	03/09/1915
War Diary	Maresquel	03/09/1915	03/09/1915
War Diary	Ain-En-Mart	04/09/1915	18/09/1915
War Diary	Lebriz	19/09/1915	21/09/1915
War Diary	Hezeques	22/09/1915	22/09/1915
War Diary	La Miqvillers	23/09/1915	24/09/1915
War Diary	Bethune	25/09/1915	25/09/1915
War Diary	Noyelles	26/09/1915	28/09/1915
War Diary	Sailly Labourse	28/09/1915	28/09/1915
War Diary	Amezen	29/09/1915	29/09/1915
War Diary	Nonent Fontes	30/09/1915	30/09/1915
Heading	24th Division Oct 15 73rd F. Ambulance Vol. 2 Oct 15		
War Diary	Nonent Fontes	01/10/1915	02/10/1915
War Diary	Herzeele	03/10/1915	06/10/1915
War Diary	Pt 720 C Sheet 27 near Proven	07/10/1915	11/10/1915
War Diary	P 5 G 34 C 7.1 Sheet 28	12/10/1915	12/10/1915
War Diary	Reninghelst	13/10/1915	31/10/1915
Heading	24th Division Nov 15 73rd F.A. Vol 3		
War Diary	Reninghelst	01/11/1915	20/11/1915
War Diary	Eecke	21/11/1915	22/11/1915
War Diary	Ochtezeele	23/11/1915	23/11/1915
War Diary	Eperlecques	24/11/1915	27/11/1915
War Diary	Houlle	28/11/1915	30/11/1915
Heading	24th Div. December 1915 73rd F A		
War Diary	Houlle	01/12/1915	31/12/1915
Heading	24th Div Jan 1916		
War Diary	Houlle	01/01/1916	07/01/1916
War Diary	Remi Siding near Poperinghe	08/01/1916	31/01/1916
Heading	73rd F.A. 24 Div. Vol 6. Feb 1916		
War Diary	Remi Siding near Poperinghe	01/02/1916	29/02/1916
Heading	73rd F.A. 24 Div Vol 7 March 1916		
War Diary	Remi Siding Poperinghe	01/03/1916	23/03/1916
War Diary	Eecke	24/03/1916	26/03/1916
War Diary	Dranoutre	27/03/1916	30/04/1916
Heading	24th Div. May 1916 no. 73 f. amb.		
War Diary	Dranoutre	01/05/1916	01/05/1916
War Diary	Hd Qrs. S.9.d.8.0. Sheet 28	02/05/1916	31/05/1916
Heading	No. 73. 7.a. June 1916		
War Diary	S.9.d. 8.0 Sheet 28	01/06/1916	30/06/1916
Heading	24th Division 73rd Field Ambulance		
Miscellaneous	Headquarters, Q. Bde. 24 Division.	31/07/1916	31/07/1916
War Diary	S.9.d.8.0 Sheet 28	01/07/1916	21/07/1916
War Diary	Fletre	22/07/1916	24/07/1916

Type	Description	Start	End
War Diary	Molliens Vidame	25/07/1916	31/07/1916
Heading	24th Div. 73rd Field Ambulance August 1916		
Miscellaneous	Headquarters Q. Bde, 24th Division.	31/08/1916	31/08/1916
War Diary	Sheet 62D 0.5 Cheteau Corbie	01/08/1916	27/08/1916
War Diary	D 30.b.3.7	28/08/1916	31/08/1916
Heading	24th Div. 73rd Field Ambulance Sept 1916		
Miscellaneous	Headquarters Q Branch 24th Division.	30/09/1916	30/09/1916
War Diary	Sheet 62D F.2.d.9.9.	01/09/1916	05/09/1916
War Diary	Lens II Bouchon	06/09/1916	19/09/1916
War Diary	Ref 36 B D25.a.24 Marles-Les-Mines	20/09/1916	23/09/1916
War Diary	Grand Servins	24/09/1916	27/09/1916
War Diary	Reference Sheet 36 B. Grand Servins	28/09/1916	30/09/1916
Heading	24th Div. 73rd Field Ambulance Oct. 1916		
War Diary	Ref. Sheet 36 B Q 34 Central Grand Servins	01/10/1916	20/10/1916
War Diary	Q 34 Central Sheet 36B Grand Servins	21/10/1916	28/10/1916
War Diary	Sheet 36 B V36 C	29/10/1916	31/10/1916
Heading	24th Div. 73rd Field Ambulance Nov. 1916		
War Diary	Sheet 36 B L.25. B.1.3 Braquemont	01/11/1916	30/11/1916
Heading	24th Div. 73rd Field Ambulance Dec 1916		
War Diary	Sheet 36 B L 25.b.2.5.	01/12/1916	31/12/1916
Heading	24th Div. 73rd Field Ambulance Jan 1917		
War Diary	Sheet 36 B L 25.b.1.3.	01/01/1917	01/01/1917
War Diary	Bracquemont	02/01/1917	31/01/1917
Heading	24th Div. 73rd Field Ambulance Feb. 1917		
War Diary	Braquemont	01/02/1917	12/02/1917
War Diary	Moeux-Les. Mines	13/02/1917	28/02/1917
Diagram etc	Evacuation Scheme 73rd Fld Amb.		
Miscellaneous	Capt. R.A.M.C.	10/02/1917	10/02/1917
Miscellaneous	73rd Field Ambulance		
Miscellaneous	73rd Field Ambulance	17/02/1917	17/02/1917
Miscellaneous	73rd Field Ambulance R.A.M.C.	24/02/1917	24/02/1917
Miscellaneous	73rd Field Ambulance	03/03/1917	03/03/1917
Heading	24th Div. 73rd Field Ambulance Mar. 1917		
War Diary	Moeux-Les-Mines	01/03/1917	02/03/1917
War Diary	Braquemont	03/03/1917	31/03/1917
Diagram etc	Line of Evacuation 73rd Field Ambulance	22/03/1917	31/03/1917
Miscellaneous	73rd Field Ambulance	01/03/1917	01/03/1917
Miscellaneous	73rd Field Ambulance.	02/03/1917	02/03/1917
Diagram etc	Sketch Plan Line of Evacuation. 73rd Field Ambulance	02/03/1917	22/03/1917
Heading	24th Div. 73rd. F.a. April 1917		
War Diary	Braquemont	01/04/1917	30/04/1917
Miscellaneous	B.E.F. Summary Of Medical War Diaries Of 73rd Field Ambulance		
War Diary	Operations Enemy, & Ops Enemy Gas.	06/04/1917	06/04/1917
War Diary	Med. Arr.	07/04/1917	08/04/1917
War Diary	Moves Det.	09/04/1917	09/04/1917
War Diary	Operations & Casualties	12/04/1917	12/04/1917
War Diary	Operations	15/04/1917	15/04/1917
War Diary	Evacuation	15/04/1917	15/04/1917
War Diary	Terrain	15/04/1917	15/04/1917
War Diary	Med. Arr.	15/04/1917	15/04/1917
War Diary		16/04/1917	16/04/1917
War Diary	Med. Arr.	17/04/1917	17/04/1917
War Diary	Evacuation & Casualties		
War Diary	Military Situation & Med. Arr.	19/04/1917	20/04/1917
War Diary	Med. Arr.	20/04/1917	20/04/1917

Diagram etc	Front Line	07/04/1919	07/04/1919
Diagram etc	Front Line	14/04/1919	14/04/1919
War Diary	Med. Arr.	20/04/1917	20/04/1917
War Diary	Transfer	21/04/1917	30/04/1917
War Diary	Operations Enemy, & Ops. Enemy Gas.	06/04/1917	06/04/1917
War Diary	Med. Arr.	07/04/1917	07/04/1917
War Diary		08/04/1917	08/04/1917
War Diary	Moves Det.	09/04/1917	09/04/1917
War Diary	Operation & Casualties	12/04/1917	12/04/1917
War Diary	Operation	14/04/1917	14/04/1917
War Diary	Med. Arr.	14/04/1917	14/04/1917
War Diary	Operations	15/04/1917	15/04/1917
War Diary	Evacuation	15/04/1917	15/04/1917
War Diary	Terrain	15/04/1917	15/04/1917
War Diary	Med. Arr.	15/04/1917	15/04/1917
War Diary		16/04/1917	16/04/1917
War Diary	Med. Arr.	17/04/1917	17/04/1917
War Diary	Evacuation & Casualties	17/04/1917	17/04/1917
War Diary	Military Situation & Med. Arr.	19/04/1917	20/04/1917
War Diary	Med. Arr.	20/04/1917	20/04/1917
War Diary	Transfer	21/04/1917	30/04/1917
Diagram etc	73rd Field Ambulance.		
Miscellaneous	The situation of "B" Section 73rd Field Ambulance and communication with our R.M. Os at 6Pm this evening are as follows.	14/04/1917	14/04/1917
Miscellaneous	Situation report 73rd Field Ambulance in front area at 6Pm this evening is as follows.	16/04/1917	16/04/1917
Diagram etc	73rd Field Ambulance.		
War Diary	73rd Field Ambulance.	19/04/1917	19/04/1917
Heading	73. F.A. May 1917		
Miscellaneous	B.E.F. Summary Of Medical War Diaries Of 73rd Field Ambulance		
War Diary	Moves	02/05/1917	09/05/1917
War Diary	Moves & Transfer	10/05/1917	10/05/1917
War Diary	Moves	02/05/1917	09/05/1917
War Diary	Moves & Transfer	10/04/1917	10/04/1917
War Diary	Braquemont	01/05/1917	01/05/1917
War Diary	Houchin	02/05/1917	07/05/1917
War Diary	Verquin	08/05/1917	08/05/1917
War Diary	Mt. Bernahon	09/05/1917	09/05/1917
War Diary	Tannay	10/05/1917	11/05/1917
War Diary	Steenvoorde	12/05/1917	13/05/1917
War Diary	Devonshire Camp Reninqhelst	14/05/1917	19/05/1917
War Diary	Devonshire Camp	20/05/1917	27/05/1917
War Diary	Hesken	28/05/1917	31/05/1917
War Diary	M 3a 59	31/05/1917	31/05/1917
Miscellaneous	Operation Orders. 73rd. Field Ambulance	14/05/1917	14/05/1917
Miscellaneous	73rd. Field Ambulance.	25/05/1917	25/05/1917
Heading	No. 73. F.A. June 1917		
War Diary	Reninghelst	01/06/1917	12/06/1917
War Diary	Map 27 R2.a.8.9	13/06/1917	15/06/1917
War Diary	R 2 a 89	16/06/1917	30/06/1917
Diagram etc	Assembly Trenches		
Operation(al) Order(s)	Operation Orders 73rd Field Ambulance.	06/06/1917	06/06/1917
Miscellaneous	A.D.M.S. 24th Divn.	09/06/1917	09/06/1917

Diagram etc	Diagram Showing Lines of Evacuation Between Regiment Aid Posts & Dressing Station, Etc.		
Heading	No. 73. F. A. July 1917		
War Diary	R 2 a 89	01/07/1917	31/07/1917
Operation(al) Order(s)	Operation Order 73rd Field Ambulance.	23/07/1917	23/07/1917
Heading	No. 73. F. A. Aug. 1917		
War Diary	R2 a89	01/08/1917	31/08/1917
Heading	No. 73 F. A. Sept. 1917		
War Diary	In The Field	01/09/1917	03/09/1917
War Diary	R 2 a89	04/09/1917	13/09/1917
War Diary	Doolieu	15/09/1917	20/09/1917
War Diary	Sheet 57 C D21 b26	21/09/1917	23/09/1917
War Diary	L 29 Central	24/09/1917	24/09/1917
War Diary	Bernes	25/09/1917	30/09/1917
Miscellaneous	73rd. Field Ambulance. Operation Order.	19/09/1917	19/09/1917
Operation(al) Order(s)	73rd. Field Ambulance. Operation Order.	23/09/1917	23/09/1917
Map			
Heading	War Diary 73rd Field Ambulance For October 1917		
War Diary	Bernes	01/10/1917	31/10/1917
Heading	War Diary 73rd Field Ambulance From Nov 1st to Nov 30th 1917		
War Diary	Bernes	01/11/1917	30/11/1917
Heading	73rd Field Ambulance R.A.M.C. War Diary for the month of December 17 Volume 28.		
War Diary	Bernes	01/12/1917	31/12/1917
Heading	73rd Field Ambulance War Diary for the month of January 1918		
War Diary	Bernes	01/01/1918	31/01/1918
Heading	73rd Field Ambulance War Diary for the month of February 1918		
War Diary	Bernes	01/02/1918	28/02/1918
Heading	War Diary (Original) 73rd Field Ambulance March 1918		
War Diary		01/03/1918	31/03/1918
Heading	73rd Field Ambulance. War Diary (Original) April 1918 Volume No. 32.		
War Diary	Saint Sauflieu	01/04/1918	03/04/1918
War Diary	Amiens	04/04/1918	06/04/1918
War Diary	Saleux		
War Diary	Valines	07/04/1918	17/04/1918
War Diary	Beugin	18/04/1918	29/04/1918
War Diary	Fosse 10	30/04/1918	30/04/1918
Heading	73 Field Ambulance. War Diary May 1918 Volume 33		
War Diary	Fosse 10	01/05/1918	31/05/1918
Diagram etc	Scheme of Evacuation Front area		
Diagram etc	Diagrammatical Plan. Gas Centre 73 Fld Ambce.		
Heading	War Diary 73rd. Field Ambulance June 1918 Volume No. 34		
War Diary	Fosse 10	01/06/1918	30/06/1918
Heading	No. 73 F. A. July 1918		
Heading	73 Field Ambulance War Diary July 1918 Volume No. 35		
War Diary	Fosse 10	01/07/1918	31/07/1918
Miscellaneous	73rd Field Ambulance.		
Heading	73 Field Ambulance War Diary August 1918 Volume No. 36		

War Diary	Fosse 10 (Sains)	01/08/1918	16/08/1918
War Diary	Grand Servins	18/08/1918	31/08/1918
Miscellaneous	73rd Field Ambulance	03/08/1918	03/08/1918
Heading	73rd Field Ambulance War Diary (Original) September 1918 Volume No. 37.		
War Diary		01/09/1918	30/09/1918
Heading	Cover for Documents. Nature of Enclosures.		
Heading	73 Field Ambulance War Diary October 1918 Vol. 38		
War Diary	Hersin Milly	01/10/1918	06/10/1918
War Diary	Havrincourt	07/10/1918	07/10/1918
War Diary	Noyelles	08/10/1918	10/10/1918
War Diary	Rumilly	10/10/1918	10/10/1918
War Diary	B8. b.8.8. (57B)	11/10/1918	14/10/1918
War Diary	Rieux	15/10/1918	16/10/1918
War Diary	Cambrai	17/10/1918	25/10/1918
War Diary	Haussy	26/10/1918	31/10/1918
Heading	73rd Field Ambulance War Diary November 1918 Volume No. 39		
War Diary	Haussy	01/11/1918	02/11/1918
War Diary	Bermerain	03/11/1918	03/11/1918
War Diary	Sepmeries	04/11/1918	04/11/1918
War Diary	Villers Pol	05/11/1918	05/11/1918
War Diary	St. Waast	07/11/1918	07/11/1918
War Diary	Bavay	08/11/1918	11/11/1918
War Diary	Wargnies	16/11/1918	16/11/1918
War Diary	Rouvignies	17/11/1918	18/11/1918
War Diary	Auberchicourt	19/11/1918	30/11/1918
Heading	73rd Field Ambulance War Diary for the month of December 1918		
War Diary	Field	01/12/1918	31/12/1918
Heading	73rd Field Ambulance R.A.M.C. War Diary for the month of January 1919		
War Diary	Field	01/01/1919	31/01/1919
Heading	73rd Field Ambulance War Diary for month of February 1919		
War Diary	Field	01/02/1919	28/02/1919
Heading	73rd Field Ambulance War Diary for the month of March 1919		
War Diary	Taintignies (Belgium)	01/03/1919	31/03/1919
Heading	73rd Field Ambulance War Diary for the month of April 1919		
War Diary	Field	01/04/1919	30/04/1919

WO/95/2202/2
73 Field Ambulance

25TH DIVISION
MEDICAL

73RD FIELD AMBULANCE
AUG 1915 - ~~DEC 1918~~
1919 APL

74th Division

Summarised 73rd Field Amb.
Vol I

121/7761

August
Sept

Aug to Sep!
Dec '18

Army Form C. 2118.

WAR DIARY
or
INTELLIGENCE SUMMARY.
(Erase heading not required.)

737A I

Place	Date	Hour	Summary of Events and Information	Remarks and references to Appendices
Eastbourne	21.8.15		Orders for mobilisation of 24th Division received. Checked all issues & Fingers Equipment	
"	22.8.15		Strength of unit made up to the following numbers 10 Officers, other ranks 182. Advance party of 1 Officer & ten men left for Bulswater Camp	
"	23.8.15		Main body left Eastbourne at 9.30am for Bulswater Camp, arrived Bulswater Camp at 2 p.m.	
Bulswater Camp	24.8.15		12 noon annual Bulswater camp. General fatigue. ASC attached and returned strength of ASC as named officer & 38 other ranks	
"	25.8.15		Inquiries made as to drawing reserve equipment. Equipment partly drawn. 15 military & 21 H.D. horse attached	
"	26.8.15		Continued to draw equipment, name taken for innoculation & vaccination	
"	27.8.15		Friday night 27.8.15 when storeroom received for use proceeding over sea	
"	28.8.15		General harness & equipment, men inoculated & vaccinated	
"	29.8.15		eighteen mules received	
"	30.8.15		General fatigue	
"	31.8.15		More equipment drawn. Information made for moving all cart equipment removed S.A.S.C. horses made up afternoon 1 early Wednesday morning	
"	1.9.15		1st July left 3.30 a.m. 2nd part at 5 a.m. entrained at Blackdown arrived Southampton arrived at 10 a.m. two hour Route to Southampton	

Army Form C. 2118

WAR DIARY
or
INTELLIGENCE SUMMARY.
(Erase heading not required.)

Place	Date	Hour	Summary of Events and Information	Remarks and references to Appendices
Southampton	1.9.15		Embarked S.S. Italian Prince USS Independence for Havre at 4 p.m. & 8 p.m. Strength eight officers 150 N.C.O.'s & men on the S.S. Italian Prince.	
Havre	2.9.15		Two officers & 171 N.C.O.'s & men. Empr Queen. All arrived safely. Laid Havre & proceeded to rest camp.	
		11.30 a.m.	Left rest camp for train.	
Havre	3.9.15		Entrained at 6 am for Amiens front. Advance men arrived out with difficult progress, billets having no ladders of loading wagon not in, the walls cunhelin was very bad. With the small low got ready before starting on the train journey. The journey throughout the day about 6 + 7.30 p.m. on	
Amiens	3.9.15		Arrived 7.30 still raining, the frustration for unloading had all with the small Alsterne men was urgent about. The unloading was with hope, 10 ambulance wagons with our own to the camp. The difficulty of unloading. The pit orders to march to the village of Amiens front.	
Amiens front	4.9.15		Arrived 1.30 a.m. into billets from the height main of the village total strength 10 officers, other ranks 220, all men have been allotted & billeted at Havre. Remarks of equipment indented for: gen. fatigue.	
	5.9.15			
	6.9.15		Got filled up in working order, than horses & mules also softening harness, in line was fit for the before travelling premises.	

WAR DIARY or INTELLIGENCE SUMMARY

Army Form C. 2118

Place	Date	Hour	Summary of Events and Information	Remarks and references to Appendices
Bon-en-Ponte	7.9.15		Seven motor ambulances arrived and capable of lifting four lying down cases. Had need to return Time reported to march from billets to crossroads on ST. OMER ROAD (time reached on form)	
"	8.9.15		General Training.	
"	9.9.15		Section picked in forming dressing stations, erecting bivouacs & extemporising shelters.	
"	10.9.15		Visited by A.D.M.S. & A.D.M.S. [?] (11th Army Corps) (26th Division). General condition satisfactory.	
"	11.9.15		A.S.C. attached handed in all arms as per written order of 11.9.15. Orders received for the moving of a Field Ambulance Hospital in lieu of cases not able to regain their Corps - details [?] 13 Section was detailed for this duty. Church parade by C of E chaplain.	
"	12.9.15		Orders received for general manoeuvres for following day.	
"	13.9.15		General manoeuvres 73rd F. Amb joined 71st Brigade at Arras. Moved about 6.15 a.m. in thunder to St Servain, orders were that the various Ambulances the full day owing to heavy rain. Returned to camp. The remainder of the day was devoted to cleaning up wagons, water carts & general fatigues.	

Army Form C. 2118.

WAR DIARY
or
INTELLIGENCE SUMMARY.
(Erase heading not required.)

Instructions regarding War Diaries and Intelligence Summaries are contained in F. S. Regs., Part II. and the Staff Manual respectively. Title pages will be prepared in manuscript.

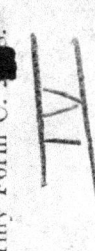

Place	Date	Hour	Summary of Events and Information	Remarks and references to Appendices
Ain in Arab	15.9.15		No special incidents to record, general training of Field Ambulance, route march	
"	16.9.15		Unit moved with reinforcements conducted on these area.	
"	17.9.15		Route march	
"	18.9.15		Unit ordered to move	
Lebig	19.9.15		Unit moved to Lebig leaving at 17.0am 3.30 a.m. B section was left behind & ordered to open on the following day. The unit was some delay during the march owing to the hilly roads & the wagons & G.S. wagons halted for 10 hours up the road have seen deep gulleys. B section rejoined the unit arriving at 11.0 am C section formed a dressing station. Escaped our medical newcomers for other two for guarding, dam't officers attended troops in their duties in the field.
"	20.9.15		Orders to move. Left at 6.30 provided with 93rd Brigade 15 mules needed. Hezequas at 11.45 p.m. 68 men held up on the way, suffering from sore feet, during return march
Hezequas	21.9.15		Received orders to move, moved with brigade 21 miles to La Maguillanie arriving at 3.15 am. 23.9.15 held up 30 men, our ambulance full strength	
	22.9.15			

2353 Wt: W23H/1451 700,000 5/15 D.D.&L. A.D.S.S./Forms/C. 2118.

Army Form C. 2118

WAR DIARY
or
INTELLIGENCE SUMMARY
(Erase heading not required.)

Instructions regarding War Diaries and Intelligence Summaries are contained in F.S. Regs, Part II and the Staff Manual respectively. Title Pages will be prepared in manuscript.

Place	Date	Hour	Summary of Events and Information	Remarks and references to Appendices
La Brispillere	23.9.15		Had a rest, the men very tired, but very cheerful, fortunately the weather has been fair though led during the day.	
"	24.9.15		Carried on the usual routine, when received orders not to be ready to move at 6 p.m. Marched 10 miles to Bethune arriving at 2.30 a.m. fell through the night.	
Bethune	25.9.15		Ordered at 12.30 mm to proceed to Noyelles, arrived at 3.30. All been outdone with three officers proceeded to get in touch with the 73rd brigade. After much difficulty, the 73rd Brigade had been allotted to 2nd Division the bearer subdivision section took with the Brigade & proceeded to collect wounded. The work was very trying to the men who were under fire for the first time & behaved with great courage.	
Noyelles	26.9.15	2 am	6 Section stretcherbearers were asked out to advanced dressing station J 29 A 7 A. Zie 41735. Pt for a.e. were out with a bearer party knee deep through the slush. One bearer was wounded in left shoulder. All had a very hard days work carrying to the different of wounded, the wounded spite enduring the work.	
Noyelles	27.9.15		Charles bearer was wounded by shrapnel in the month whilst carrying wounded. C. Gunsttmann relieved by 23 Gunsttmann, another very hard day's fighting	

Army Form C. 2118

WAR DIARY
or
INTELLIGENCE SUMMARY
(Erase heading not required.)

Instructions regarding War Diaries and Intelligence Summaries are contained in F. S. Regs., Part II. and the Staff Manual respectively. Title Pages will be prepared in manuscript.

Place	Date	Hour	Summary of Events and Information	Remarks and references to Appendices
Noyelles	26.9.15		13 F.A. settlemen relieved by a C.C.S. settlemen at 9.30 a.m. Large numbers of wounded passing through about obtained. Stretcher attached to Vermelles. Later received that ambulance was to be relieved, when given four stills T.A. to follow 73rd Brigade marched to field near Sailly Labourse & bivouacked night very hot, no arrangements made by Brigade for suitable camping ground.	
Sailly Labourse	28.9.15		Ordered to move about 9 p.m. in great difficulty in getting transport in pitchy darkness, men very tired field owing to the mud & darkness.	
Annezin	29.9.15		Arrived very late (and great difficulty in getting billets, eventually got men under cover in billets & gave disposition for Officers. Men bivouac'd about 11.30 a.m. & marched to Hourel Jardin.	
Hourd Jardin	30.9.15		Started a heavy station & extracted a few act of the Brigade most suffering from sore feet.	

W.G. Mauflyn
Lieutenant Colonel
O.C. 73rd Field Ambulance

Oct 1915

34th Division

73rd F. Ambulance
vol: 2

19/12/77

Oct 15.

and

WAR DIARY or INTELLIGENCE SUMMARY

Army Form C. 2118

Place	Date	Hour	Summary of Events and Information	Remarks and references to Appendices
Lestrem Gorre	1.10.15		The day employed in enemy's the loading of the waggons, the transport was ordered to proceed by road to a new area.	
" "	2.10.15		Received orders for entraining. Unit advanced party left at 4.30 a.m. Proceeded by rail for BERGUETTE to GODEWAERSVELDE, the main body left at 11.15 a.m. proceeded to the same route, marching from there to HERZEELE a distance of ten miles arriving about 6.30 p.m. A Section found a hospital in a chateau which was a very suitable place that been used for German prisoners by some other unit.	
HERZEELE	3.10.15		General inspection of the unit by the A.D.C. 24th Division at 10 a.m. the A.D.C. commented much by the A.D.C. was that the hospital arrived sortt in walker from another, this is not be employed ?at owing to the highly low landment weather of the country.	
"	4.10.15		First intent from on the 6th F.S.A.C. containing allotted to 5th Division	
"	5.10.15		Church parade.	
"	6.10.15		Received orders from L/A HERZEELE at 1 p.m. and marched with 73rd Brigade arrived at Point 720.C. Shelf 27 near PROVEN filled my tents to obtain got 60 men under canvas in bivouac places in tent in field. Sources all looks well must in order to prevent detection of aeroplanes	
Pt 720 C Sheet 27 near PROVEN	7.10.15		Continued staining tents pitched a small hospital for out of brigade, ready cases of one feet.	
"	8.10.15		Field equipment & vehicles for efficiency	
"	9.10.15		Routine inspection of unit	
"	10.10.15		Church Parade	
"	11.10.15		Left camp at 9.30 a.m. Proceeded with 73rd Brigade via POPERINGHE to RENINGHELST arriving at 12.45 encamped at Point G.34.C.11 sheet 28 and halt in field which used for the Ministrion of the officers in limbs, this is difficulty in getting water, water cart harms to go three miles every day to the nearest

1875 Wt. W503/826 1,000,000 4/15 J.B.C. & A. A.D.S.S./Forms/C 2118.

WAR DIARY or INTELLIGENCE SUMMARY

Army Form C. 2118

(Erase heading not required.)

Place	Date	Hour	Summary of Events and Information	Remarks and references to Appendices
RENINGHELST	12.10.15		Hospital closed & all out beds over to the 73rd Field Amb.	
"	13.10.15		On orders asked to take over advanced dressing station provided by OUDERDOM & Estab. an on the following day from the 28th Fd Amb., also an Aid post for the 27th A at Dickebusch H	
"	14.10.15		Took over huts from 217A + 217A	
"	15.10.15		General arranging of camp, building, excavation on frontage. Use other for cricket.	
"	16.10.15		Men employed in thickening hts under direction of Belgian workmen.	
"	17.10.15		Stands made.	
"	18.10.15		Latrines erected & trenches forward to same huts.	
"	19.10.15		Examined buildings huts for Officers men already under own & Hotels &c.	
"	20.10.15		Found & Belgian	
"	21.10.15		Shortage of water, started to make a satisfying ground for heavy trenches.	
"	22.10.15		The amount of water built & found to be very satisfactory.	
"	23.10.15		More kitchen supplied & erected in the rest of building huts, the walls is far but cold.	
"	24.10.15		Stands Parade.	
"	25.10.15		Weather very bad, arrangements carried on with building huts.	
"	26.10.15		Weather still very bad the condition of the roads near the camp very bad, fatigue parties employed repairing part of the roads also, building huts, parades & making standings for the horses.	

Army Form C.2118

WAR DIARY
or
INTELLIGENCE SUMMARY

(Erase heading not required.)

Place	Date	Hour	Summary of Events and Information	Remarks and references to Appendices
RELINGHELST	27.10.15		His Majesty the King visited the trenches on this day. A detachment under an Officer were present at the ceremonial parade. His Majesty informed his approval of the appearance of the 2nd Army.	
"	28.10.15		Weather wet. Work consists of camp in very wet muddy, general fatigues.	
"	29.10.15		Building of huts proceeding satisfactorily.	
"	30.10.15		General fatigues, we are hut about completed.	
"	31.10.15		Church Parade.	

W.G. Maydon
Major. R.A.M.C.
OFFICER COMMANDING
73RD FIELD AMB., 24TH DIVISION.

J H Worsum

73rd F.A.
Tot. 3

121/7624

Nov. 15.

Nov 1915

Army Form C. 2118

WAR DIARY
or
INTELLIGENCE SUMMARY
(Erase heading not required.)

Instructions regarding War Diaries and Intelligence Summaries are contained in F.S. Regs., Part II and the Staff Manual respectively. Title Pages will be prepared in manuscript.

Place	Date	Hour	Summary of Events and Information	Remarks and references to Appendices
RENINGHELST	Nov 2.15		Weather still very wet. Fatigues providing standing cases & difficulty in getting wood.	
"	3rd		Relief party at OUDERDOM relieved.	
"	4th		Weather still bad. The company general went out to mud. DICKEBUSHE party relieved.	
"	5th		General fatigues & building of huts continued.	
"	6th		General fatigues	
"	7th		17th Brigade took over part of the line towards the South of YPRES. Belfast House to the [...] by 24th Division.	
"	8th		Orders received to take over BEDFORD House, two officers & two huts, also two men from 2/5 7.A.	
"	9th		General fatigues	
"	10th		Another Sergt & four men detailed for duty at BEDFORD House.	
"	11th		A supply of 3500 bricks turned from C.R.E. for purpose of completing huts standings. All building stopped owing to lack of material, men [...] few now left two owing to heavy fire observed trans[...] stations. Last [...] to YPRES & farm rubble for making roads wagon.	
"	12th		Weather still very wet & cold. Company convoy made for purpose of stables.	
"	13th		Very wet. All building operations suspended. Supplies at BRASSERIE & BEDFORD House finished.	
"	14th		Church parade	
"	15th		General fatigues	
"	16th			

Army Form C. 2118

WAR DIARY
or
INTELLIGENCE SUMMARY
(Erase heading not required.)

Instructions regarding War Diaries and Intelligence Summaries are contained in F. S. Regs., Part II. and the Staff Manual respectively. Title Pages will be prepared in manuscript.

Place	Date	Hour	Summary of Events and Information	Remarks and references to Appendices
RENINGHLEST	17.11.15		Weather very wet & unfavorable to perform any work in camp.	
"	18.11.15		Building operations continued, still a lack of timber.	
"	19.11.15		Received orders to relieve party at BEDFORD HOUSE.	
"	20.11.15		OUDERDOM and DICKIEBUSHE parties relieved on a temporary measure by 92 F.A. at out p.m. and left RENINGHLEST after being relieved by 142nd F.A. 3rd Division & marched [?] in rear of 73rd Infantry Brigade to EECKE arriving there at 11.30 P.M. Weather very good but cold.	
EECKE	21.11.15		Units rested for the day.	
"	22.11.15		Unit left EECKE at 10 a.m. and marched with Brigade to OCHTEZEELE arriving at 3.30 P.M.	
OCHTEZEELE	23.11.15		Unit left OCHTEZEELE travelled with Brigade to not billets arriving at EPERLECQUES at 4.33 P.M. The unit billeted for one hour en route for lunch. Weather fine.	
EPERLECQUES	24.11.15		General fatigues. Found Hospital for reception of sick, harnesses, Field S[?] orderly hours under cover.	
"	25.11.15		Two horse ambulance wagons sent out to follow Brigade who moved further on to meet returns for 71st & 72nd Brigades.	
"	26.11.15		General fatigues.	
"	27.11.15		Received orders to move to new billets at HOUILLE. Unit reached new billets at 11o'c, all billets found.	
HOUILLE	28.11.15		Settled in billets, horses under cover. General fatigues. Three parade slung packed to meet at all officers kits up for night.	
"	29.11.15		General fatigues. Instructed all Waterman L.Cl for deficiencies. Found a detachment hospital.	
"	30.11.15		General fatigue and general refilling, cleaning & retaining waggons where necessary.	

J. G. Meiklejohn
R.A.M.C.
OFFICER COMMANDING
73rd FIELD AMB, 24TH DIVISION.

73rd FA.
Vol: 4

76/7936

24th ☒

F/140/1

73rd FA

December 1915

Army Form C. 2118

Instructions regarding War Diaries and Intelligence Summaries are contained in F.S. Regs., Part II and the Staff Manual respectively. Title Pages will be prepared in manuscript.

WAR DIARY
or
INTELLIGENCE SUMMARY

(Erase heading not required.)

Place	Date	Hour	Summary of Events and Information	Remarks and references to Appendices
HOUlLE	1.12.15		Unit in rest billets. Sick on collected duty for Brigade and attended in Field ambulance of rest conducted nursing. reports to C.C.S. Regiment II under instructions of A.D.M.S. every three days in advance. Very rainy weather, not cold	
"	2.12.15		General fatigues, cleaning & ridding of horses & wagons. Still wet	
"	3.12.15		Fitting, material & transport equipment. Another review	
"	4.12.15		Finishing material & transport equipment. Raining hard, roads very muddy	
"	5.12.15		Church parade.	
"	6.12.15		Sorting of stores equipment	
"	7.12.15		Lt. Col. Procter & Lieutenant in antigas measures. General exempt of ambulance	
"	8.12.15		Route march. General fatigues.	
"	9.12.15		First supplies for holding manoeuvres. These held owing to the field being overtaxed, two performances 10/11. Four men transferred away to cover of tubercular invalids at base depot ROUEN.	
"	10.12.15		Weather very mild, general fatigues.	
"	11.12.15		Church parade.	
"	12.12.15		Issue of new clothing, kit inspection.	
"	13.12.15		Squad & stretcher drill.	
"	14.12.15		General fatigues, cleaning of wagons.	
"	15.12.15		General fatigues, lectures by certain officers in Field Ambulance work.	
"	16.12.15		General fatigues, route march.	
"	17.12.15		Field ambulance drill, fatigues.	
"	18.12.15		Church parade.	
"	19.12.15		Fatigues, route march.	
"	20.12.15		Shelter drill, fatigues.	
"	21.12.15		General fatigues, weather wet & stormy	

WAR DIARY
or
INTELLIGENCE SUMMARY
(Erase heading not required.)

Army Form C. 2118

Instructions regarding War Diaries and Intelligence Summaries are contained in F. S. Regs., Part II. and the Staff Manual respectively. Title Pages will be prepared in manuscript.

Place	Date	Hour	Summary of Events and Information	Remarks and references to Appendices
Houlle	23.12.15		Route march, general fatigues	
"	24.12.15		Issued fatigues parties in use of gas helmets	
"	25.12.15		Church Parade.	
"	26.12.15		Lecture on aids to prevention.	
"	27.12.15		Route march, kit inspection.	
"	28.12.15		Issued fatigues, wagon drill.	
"	29.12.15		Inspection by F.O.C. Division performed at the last moment, when he say on general duties	
"	30.12.15		Route march, general fatigues.	
"	31.12.15		Inspected by F.O.C. Division who expressed himself as being very pleased with the appearance of the men, the turnout of the transport was also satisfactory.	

W.G. Maydon, Major
R.A.M.C.
O.C. 73rd F.A.
OFFICER COMMANDING
73RD FIELD AMB., 24TH DIVISION.

73 F.A.
Vol. 5

24th Div.

F/140/2.

73 F.A

Jan 1916

Army Form C. 2118

WAR DIARY
or
INTELLIGENCE SUMMARY
(Erase heading not required.)

Instructions regarding War Diaries and Intelligence Summaries are contained in F. S. Regs., Part II. and the Staff Manual respectively. Title Pages will be prepared in manuscript.

Place	Date	Hour	Summary of Events and Information	Remarks and references to Appendices
HOULLE	1.1.16		Unit still in rest billets, general fatigues.	
"	2.1.16		Church parade.	
"	3.1.16		General fatigues, preparations being made for move, huts collecting, repaired by night.	
"	4.1.16		Advance party of one officer & fin. & C.O. men left for POPERINGE to take over Divisional Rest Station.	
"	5.1.16		Two officers and one other rank proceeded to REMI Siding to take over Divisional Rest Station. All transport left to Divisional Rest Station.	
"	6.1.16		Main body of Field Ambulance left HOULLE, two sections marched to AUDRUICQ & entrained the, another section entrained at WATTEN both arrived at REMI SIDING on the same day.	
REMI SIDING	8.1.16		General fatigues cleaning of billets & revamping camp, one ophed transport men left for Divisional Rest POPERINGHE.	
nr POPERINGHE	9.1.16		General fatigues, party from District received into Divisional Rest Station. Party of R.E. engaged in fitting huts for blinds.	
"	10.1.16		Two wards fully extended & arranged to receive cases.	
"	11.1.16		General fatigues.	
"	12.1.16		Part of Divisional men detailed for duty with No. 11 C.C.S. lately eighteen men returned from Divisional Baths.	
"	13.1.16		General fatigues, daily sound of sick average forty.	
"	14.1.16		General fatigues, inmates of Poperinghe.	
"	15.1.16		Sunday, a short form for the evening Read t. General fatigues	
"	16.1.16		Church parade, general fatigues	
"	17.1.16		General fatigues	
"	18.1.16		Church of Eng. form & tent during but for men of Field Ambulance	
"	19.1.16		Building huts for officers also harnessing refilling.	
"	20.1.16		Building, harness cleaning refilling.	

Army Form C. 2118.

WAR DIARY
or
INTELLIGENCE SUMMARY
(Erase heading not required.)

Instructions regarding War Diaries and Intelligence Summaries are contained in F.S. Regs., Part II. and the Staff Manual respectively. Title pages will be prepared in manuscript.

Place	Date	Hour	Summary of Events and Information	Remarks and references to Appendices
REMI S.OING nr OTHERMISNE	21.1.16		General fatigues arranging Divisional Rest Station. Had boards thrown & laid to all the huts.	
"	22.1.16		Church Parade.	
"	23.1.16		Forming room on being built for use of the R.O.M.C personnel.	
"	24.1.16		General fatigues. Building of latrines for the sick preceding.	
"	25.1.16		General fatigues. Latrines being built for R.A.M.C personnel.	
"	26.1.16		Arranging of drainage scheme for drawing camp, clearing of all the round camp.	
"	27.1.16		D.R.S. inspected by D.M.S. 2nd Army, who was pleased with progress of work.	
"	28.1.16		General fatigues, new drainage system finished.	
"	29.1.16		Church Parade.	
"	30.1.16		General fatigues, making of roads & entrance to D.R.S Tents.	
"	31.1.16			N.L. Meyston Major O.C. 13 ~ F.A.

73rd F. A.
24 Div
Vol. 6

Feb 1916
S

WAR DIARY
or
INTELLIGENCE SUMMARY.

Army Form C. 2118.

(Erase heading not required.)

Place	Date	Hour	Summary of Events and Information	Remarks and references to Appendices
REMI SIDING near POPERINGHE	1.2.16		A party of 15 R.E. reported to carry out drainage schemes. The usual routine of fatigues carried out.	
"	2.2.16		Weather better, material received for building new hut for use of patients.	
"	3.2.16		Roads very rough and wet, another hut being built.	
"	4.2.16		S.O.C. division visited the D.R.S. and expressed himself as very pleased with the general arrangements.	
"	5.2.16		Weather very wet, general duties and fatigues.	
"	6.2.16		Road further general fatigues	
"	7.2.16		One hut completed and occupied by patients.	
"	8.2.16		General fatigues and road making, cutting drains.	
"	9.2.16		Arrangements made for putting water supply level on.	
"	10.2.16		Outside of huts painted.	
"	11.2.16		Very wet, general duties.	
"	12.2.16		Another hut finished and occupied by patients. The make total bed accommodation of patients two hundred.	
"	13.2.16		Road handle, 60 metre ambulance car O.72 F.A. to comrade wounded.	
"	14.2.16		Very miserable cold, general fatigues digging drains for water supply under extension of R.E.	
"	15.2.16		Lieut Mitchell attached for Company duty, work of Royal Engineers killed in action.	
"	16.2.16		General fatigues, road making, procceeding slowly	

WAR DIARY or INTELLIGENCE SUMMARY

Army Form C. 2118.

(Erase heading not required.)

Place	Date	Hour	Summary of Events and Information	Remarks and references to Appendices
REMI SIDING POPERINGHE	17.2.16		General fatigues and aerial activity during the night	
"	18.2.16		Weather very rough, general fatigues. D.R.S. emptied of sugar beet at Coyle.	
"	19.2.16		Weather better, sand men & horse killed & injured by aerial bomb dropped at 5.0 from near their camp.	
"	20.2.16		Horse R.A.M.C. reinforcements reported for duty. Church parade, sand hostile aircraft near camp.	
"	21.2.16		No enemy show.	
"	21.2.16		General fatigues, inspected lots of units also men return from Liherts.	
"	22.2.16		Baths completed, and now in full working order. From A.S.C. M.T. state transferred to base	
"			General Fatigues	
"	23.2.16		Sent fall 7 men down to the water. General fatigues	
"	24.2.16		General fatigues	
"	25.2.16		Further fall of snow, very cold.	
"	26.2.16		Two A.S.C. M.T. taken on the strength as supplies driven under new scale. Were and in	
"			very cold & disagreeable.	
"			Weather cold & stormy. Church parade, general fatigues. A. 70 X. H.E. transferred	
"	27.2.16		to No 2 F. Amb they B. Batten & about of strength. D. STEWART taken on the strength	
"	28.2.16		General fatigues and undergoing for shelter	
"	29.2.16		General fatigues, XmCC ambulance transit wanted & received by ambulance wagon. N°4 May Eng L. O.C. 73 nd F. Ambulance	

73rd F.A
24 D³
Vol 1

March 1916
April 1916

COMMITTEE FOR THE
MEDICAL HISTORY OF THE WAR
Date 9 JUN 1916

WAR DIARY
or
INTELLIGENCE SUMMARY

(Erase heading not required.)

Army Form C. 2118.

Place	Date	Hour	Summary of Events and Information	Remarks and references to Appendices
REME SIDING POPERINGHE	1.3.16		Wet & still raining. 24th Equipment Park Company, Bulk car now in full working order, but steam boiler acts very well, all now got at least two boilers having steam supply in D.N.S. Water is now much drier and milder.	
"	2.3.16		General fatigues, heavy drizzle very cloudy.	
"	3.3.16		General fatigues, hire out equipment repair to work.	
"	4.3.16		Very wet & stormy, general fatigues	
"	5.2.16		Still very wet, general fatigues	
"			Thaw & heavy further fall of snow, terrible weather, typed 40 pairs over each but now driving off by intense cold from.	
"	6.3.16		Snow, full of snow. General fatigues.	
"	7.3.16		General fatigues, weather very wet & stormy.	
"	8.3.16		Continues wet & misty	
"	9.2.16		General fatigues, no O.S.C. brew take in strength transferred from 196 to O.S.C.	
"	10.3.16		General fatigues	
"	11.3.16		Weather much milder. Their one Sergt & five men R.N.C. reinforcements arrived taken on strength	
"	12.3.16		Fine and favorable. Weather much brighter & warmer.	
"	13.2.16		General fatigues.	
"	14.3.16		General fatigues.	
"	15.2.16		D.R.S inspected by D.D.M.S. 5th Corps.	

WAR DIARY
or
INTELLIGENCE SUMMARY.
(Erase heading not required.)

Army Form C. 2118.

Instructions regarding War Diaries and Intelligence Summaries are contained in F. S. Regs., Part II. and the Staff Manual respectively. Title pages will be prepared in manuscript.

Place	Date	Hour	Summary of Events and Information	Remarks and references to Appendices
REMI SIDING				
Poperinghe	16.2.16		Captured and rainy. Weather warm and brighter.	
"	17.2.16		General fatigue parties received to mend and build new area	
"	18.3.16		Advance party of 15 men Canadian Field Ambulance arrived to assist with working of D.R.S.	
"	19.3.16		Fluid parade.	
"	20.2.16		The number of patients in D.R.S. gradually reduced before arrival of relieving Field Ambulance	
"	21.3.16		General inlier & fatigues.	
"	22.3.16		Loading wagons. General fatigues.	
"	23.3.16		Handed over D.R.S. to N.V. Canadian Field Ambulance and left for EECKE at 1.30 marching with 12th Infantry Brigade. Arrived EECKE 6.45 P.M.	
EECKE	24.3.16		Heavy fall of snow, men billeted in barns, a walls helped speed few men small advanced party sent in to DRANOUTRE.	
"	25.3.16		Weather cold & stormy. General arrangements made for collecting sick of Brigade.	
"	26.2.16		Church parade.	
DRANOUTRE	27.3.16		A.Y.C. vehicle left EECKE at 9 a.m. marched to DRANOUTRE arriving at 3.45 P.M. 16th was relieved	
"			during afternoon and advanced during 26th from No 1 Canadian Field Ambulance	
"	28.3.16		Inspected advanced dressing stations, very few patients coming in.	

Army Form C. 2118.

WAR DIARY
or
INTELLIGENCE SUMMARY

(Erase heading not required.)

Instructions regarding War Diaries and Intelligence Summaries are contained in F. S. Regs., Part II. and the Staff Manual respectively. Title pages will be prepared in manuscript.

Place	Date	Hour	Summary of Events and Information	Remarks and references to Appendices
DRANOUTRE	29.3.16		Moved into large buildings for chemis station.	
"	30.3.16		Orders received that men bathe at NEUVE EGLISE also small arid clothier and Blmt Map 28 T.2.0.c.	
"	31.3.16		B section ordered to join line from EECKE this completes the move.	

W Smythe Lt Col
O C 13th F.A.

73. I Corps
Vol 8
Army Form C. 2118.

WAR DIARY
or
INTELLIGENCE SUMMARY
(Erase heading not required.)

Instructions regarding War Diaries and Intelligence Summaries are contained in F. S. Regs., Part II. and the Staff Manual respectively. Title pages will be prepared in manuscript.

Place	Date	Hour	Summary of Events and Information	Remarks and references to Appendices
DRANOUTRE	1.4.16		Co officer debated an officer to look at DRANOUTRE and NEUVE EGLISE shewing station where arranged accommodation of troops	
"	2.4.16		Church parade. general fatigues	
"	3.4.16		General fatigues. cleaning drains & surroundings of camp, building incinerators	
"	4.4.16		Lieut BRIDGEMAN reported to detachment on termination of contract & board of officers	
"	5.4.16		General fatigues. Weather dry	
"	6.4.16		2nd Lt GOUGH reported to us arrived for duty with the unit & taken on the strength	
"	7.4.16		General fatigues. weather conditions good.	
"	8.4.16		General fatigues	
"	9.4.16		General fatigues	
"	10.4.16		Weather warm and dry. 2 O.R's of 1/4th S infantry shewing alteration who received fifteen men re-allocated for fatigue with Royal Engineers	
"	11.4.16		Received material for building TARRANT HUT, weather wet and colder	
"	12.4.16		2nd Lt S. Wood & men kept busy getting huts & moveable floor cells to the ground.	
"	13.4.16		All Leave cancelled from on home, unroofed Sgt FODEN complete written	
"	14.4.16		A hurricane THRESH hut in place of FODEN complete	
"	15.4.16		Weather wet & stormy arm from accommodation huts on C,7 & I Brigade HQ gardens	

2353 Wt. W.2341/1434 700,000 5/15 D.D. & L.   A.D.S.S./Forms/C. 2118.

Army Form C. 2118.

WAR DIARY
or
INTELLIGENCE SUMMARY.
(Erase heading not required.)

Instructions regarding War Diaries and Intelligence Summaries are contained in F. S. Regs., Part II. and the Staff Manual respectively. Title pages will be prepared in manuscript.

Place	Date	Hour	Summary of Events and Information	Remarks and references to Appendices
DRANOUTRE	16.4.16		Church parade. D.R.S. released and received number of old returned to Field Ambulance accompanied very limited.	
"	17.4.16		Very wet & stormy. Lieut LLOYD left for England intending for instruct.	
"	18.4.16		All men recalled from leave have reported their arrival. L.R. Scotland.	
"	19.4.16		Weather very wet & stormy. Captain PLAYFAIR relieved Lt STEWART at advanced dressing station.	
"	20.4.16		General duties and fatigues. Lieut GOUGH relieved Lieut KNIGHT at advanced dressing station	
"	21.4.16		General duties, weather very wet.	
"	22.4.16		Weather very wet & stormy. Lieut BRISCO detailed for latrine duty with 9th Royal SUSSEX from R.A.M.C. reinforcements reported from base depot	
"	23.4.16		Weather fine.	
"	24.4.16		General duties. Lieut Knight relieved Capt Playfair at advanced dressing station	
"	25.4.16		Weather very warm. General duties.	
"	26.4.16		General duties	
"	27.4.16		Lt Col Thayson departed on leave to England. General duties	
"	28.4.16		General duties. Small party detailed to prepare new camp at Sq 2 80. H4 S 28	

WAR DIARY
or
INTELLIGENCE SUMMARY.

Army Form C. 2118.

Place	Date	Hour	Summary of Events and Information	Remarks and references to Appendices
DRANOUTRE	29.4.18		General Notices	
	30.4.18		Received Op Ord 9 Stand to at 2.30 AM. Very heavy bombardment commenced at 4. 1 A.M. Moving order cancelled. over 350 Cases received and evacuated from 3.30 A.M. to 12. noon. 226 cases & 900 prisoners.	

K Clayton
Capt
R.A.M.C.
A/C OFFICER COMMANDING
73RD FIELD AMB., 24TH DIVISION.

24th Div.

No. 73 F. Amb.

May 1916.

T3 FORE
Army Form C. 2118.
Vol 4

WAR DIARY
or
INTELLIGENCE SUMMARY.
(Erase heading not required.)

Instructions regarding War Diaries and Intelligence Summaries are contained in F.S. Regs., Part II. and the Staff Manual respectively. Title pages will be prepared in manuscript.

Place	Date	Hour	Summary of Events and Information	Remarks and references to Appendices
DRANOUTRE	1.5.16		Continual flow of wounded and gassed cases received during PM. early morning. Very few cases received after 11 AM and Dressing Station closed by 2.0 P.M. HeadQuarters moved from DRANOUTRE to Sqd 2 O Rot 28 during the afternoon. Party of 2 Officers and 30 other Ranks left to carry on the work at Dressing Station.	
Hd.Q.R.S. Sqd 2 O. Rot 28	2.5.16		Lieut J. B. DALTON reported for duty and taken on the Strength	
	3.5.16		Preparations made at Hd Qrs for the receiving sick	
	4.5.16		Patients received at Hd Qrs from Dressing Station. Small Post Mortem opened	
	5.5.16		Car of Medical agents and Staff sent up to HP. to collect field staff sent up to replace those L.RAMC personnel reporting for duty from ROUEN Base Depot. (G.E. Reinforcements)	
	6.5.16		General Duties	
	7.5.16		General Duties. Lieut Col. MARDON returned from leave	
	8.5.16		Lieut Col. MARDON took over temporary duties as A.D.M.S. (A.D.M.S. on leave)	
	9.5.16		1 Pte A.S.C. reinforcement reported for duty. Lieut RUDKIN left for ENGLAND on leave	
	10.5.16		General Duties. 1 Pte A.S.C. reinforcement reported for duty	
	11.5.16		General Duties	

WAR DIARY
or
INTELLIGENCE SUMMARY

Army Form C. 2118.

Place	Date	Hour	Summary of Events and Information	Remarks and references to Appendices
H.Q. Steenbecque	12.5.16		General duties	
Sq. Rd.	13.5.16		General duties	
"	14.5.16		General duties. Lieut. & Qm. COCHRAN departed to ENGLAND on leave	
"	15.5.16		Advanced Dressing Station fitted up in an old Farm, emergency. 17 personnel Surgeon (V.Capt. proper) fitted up for use in Advanced Dressing Station and Field Ambulance. Def out at A.D. post. Party 9.30 two N.C.Os + 1 officer detailed & ready to proceed at a moment's notice to be occupancy. Advanced Dressing Station. N.33.c.97. Ref.7.72.	
"	16.5.16		General duties.	
"	17.5.16		A.P.M.S. 24 Division returned from leave. Lt.Col W. G. MAYDON resumed command of Field Ambulance. Lt. W. J. KNIGHT and No 49517 Sergt. J. T. SHEE of Strood awarded Military Cross and Military Medal respectively.	
"	18.5.16		General routine. Enemy's aeroplanes (2) each at heal grounded.	
"	19.5.16		General duties. Weather fine, very cold at night.	
"	20.5.16		General duties, very few sick or wounded.	
"	21.5.16		General duties.	
"	22.5.16		General duties.	

WAR DIARY
or
INTELLIGENCE SUMMARY.

Army Form C. 2118.

Place	Date	Hour	Summary of Events and Information	Remarks and references to Appendices
Headquarters 9nd 2 8 S.A. E.O.	23.5.16		Inspection of Gas Helmets & rain return. Lieut A.A.E. NEWITH returned from Gas and attached for instructional purposes to A.S.C M.T. drivers reported for duty from 72nd 7A.	
"	24.5.16		Inspected by G.O.C. 24 to Brigade and A.D.M.S. 2/Lieut NEWITH proceeded to A.D.S. Ruhr & 24 Gov S.H.	
"	25.5.16		24 Gov S.H. proceeded to A.D.S. general duties.	
"	26.5.16		One A.S.C M.T. driver reported from 74th 7A. Staff Major WARICK A.S. Corps to be on duty and later on the transfer.	
"	27.5.16		Two R.A.M.C. privates reported for duty from Base depot.	
"	28.5.16		General routine, weather good, very chilly at night.	
"	29.5.16		Inoculation of Medical return by G.O.C. 2nd Army.	
"	30.5.16		Rain during the night, cloudy, mud everywhere, general routine, number of sick & wounded decreasing.	
"	31.5.16		Very warm, general routine, Captain DALTON Lieutenant attached to 13th MIDDLESEX for duty.	

W. Murphen
T.P.C.L.
O.C. 13th 7A

No. 73 F.A.

June 1916.

S/

COMMITTEE FOR THE
MEDICAL HISTORY OF THE WAR
Date   5 AUG. 1915

Army Form C. 2118.

73 FA Amb
Roc June Vol 10

WAR DIARY
or
INTELLIGENCE SUMMARY.
(Erase heading not required.)

Instructions regarding War Diaries and Intelligence Summaries are contained in F. S. Regs. Part II. and the Staff Manual respectively. Title pages will be prepared in manuscript.

Place	Date	Hour	Summary of Events and Information	Remarks and references to Appendices
S 9.d.8.0 Sheet 28	1.6.16		General routine.	
"	2.6.16		General routine.	
"	3.6.16		One officer & fifty others ranks proceeded to A.D.S. as a reinforcement in action for an attack which had been arranged. They were not required as attack was postponed.	
"	4.6.16		Rest & reconstitution of Rest Garden, Thick fends.	
"	5.6.16		General routine, weather very cold & wet.	
"	6.6.16		General routine.	
"	7.6.16		Weather much warmer.	
"	8.6.16		General routine, fine but very chilly at night.	
"	9.6.16		N.C.O.'s were instructed in gas helmet drill.	
"	10.6.16		General routine, weather again wet and cold, some thunder.	
"	11.6.16		Church Parade, General routine	
"	12.6.16		General routine.	
"	13.6.16		Weather very wet, 6 party from officers & bustsmen attended memorial service for Lord KITCHENER at ORANGE TRE.	
"	14.6.16		General routine.	
"	15.6.16		Weather much milder, very cold at night, General routine, pneumonia cellulitis 2nd Y, removed to Colonial Hosts mary in divisional area.	

Army Form C. 2118.

WAR DIARY
or
INTELLIGENCE SUMMARY
(Erase heading not required.)

Instructions regarding War Diaries and Intelligence Summaries are contained in F. S. Regs., Part II. and the Staff Manual respectively. Title pages will be prepared in manuscript.

Place	Date	Hour	Summary of Events and Information	Remarks and references to Appendices
S.9.D.8.0 Sheet 2 P	16.6.16		General routine. First shell arrived at 4 P.M.	
"	17.6.16		Enemy shell put at 12.10 a.m. and his resume of batty of one officer & fifty men with shell dispatched to reinforce A.D.S. at 4.30 which is cancelled. General wounded commenced to arrive at A.D.S. at 4 a.m. a total of 125 wounded & 127 gas cases admitted & evacuated up to 12 noon. Gas cases & a few wounded continued to arrive during afternoon & evening.	
"	18.6.16		A total of 277 gas cases admitted & evacuated from 12 noon 17.6.16 to 6 a.m. 18.6.16 after which the D.S. & A.D.S. in turn of wounded & gassed cases. No of not wounded admitted probably round offhand for cases admitted during the day	
"	19.6.16		General routine.	
"	20.6.16		General routine. Weather fine mind warmer.	
"	21.6.16		General routine	
"	22.6.16		General routine	
"	23.6.16		General routine. A.D.S. received one slightly wounded.	
"	24.6.16		General routine	
"	25.6.16		General routine	
"	26.6.16		General routine	
"	27.6.16		General routine, very wet.	

Army Form C. 2118.

WAR DIARY
or
INTELLIGENCE SUMMARY.
(Erase heading not required.)

Place	Date	Hour	Summary of Events and Information	Remarks and references to Appendices
59 D.E.D Shot 2F	26.6.16		One Officer 46 Other ranks detailed to proceed to A.D.S. Dead in entertaining trains.	
" "	29.6.16		93 wounded admitted & evacuated at 6 a.m. One wounded German prisoner in above included 7A.	
" "	30.6.16		116 wounded admitted & evacuated at 10 A.M. evacuation from	

30.6.16

J.J. Maynard
O.C. 73" 7 A

24th Division

73rd Field Ambulance

July 1916

To:
Headquarters,
    A Bch 24 Division,

Herewith Original copy of War Diary for July.

Please acknowledge receipt hereon.

[signature]

Lt Col R.A.M.O.
OFFICER COMMANDING
73RD FIELD AMB., TH DIVISION.

F.A.3.
31.7.16

24 Lun
Army Form C. 2118.

73 J. and

WAR DIARY
or
INTELLIGENCE SUMMARY
(Erase heading not required.)

Vol 17

Place	Date	Hour	Summary of Events and Information	Remarks and references to Appendices
59.D.8.0 Sheet 28	1.7.16		One officer & eleven other ranks left Kandahar Farm ADS & took over ADS Lindenhoek from 7th F.A.	
"	2.7.16		General routine weather fine.	
"	3.7.16		Handed over Neuve Eglise fell to Australians F.A. Moved over 50th Division Balk ad Locre.	
"	4.7.16		All went relieved at Kandahar Farm & handed over ADS to Australian F.A.S.	
"	5.7.16		General routine	
"	6.7.16		General routine	
"	7.7.16		General routine	
"	8.7.16		Orders received to take over ADS at Kandahar Farm. and also Neuve Eglise & the Advguards of the unit upon recently at camp handed over by V Australian F.A.	
"	9.7.16		All posts & ADS as usual	
"	10.7.16			
"	11.7.16		3 officers wounded admitted from 4 AM to 10 a.m.	
"	12.7.16		General routine	
"	13.7.16		One officer & eighteen other ranks attached & returned & took over ADS at Lindenhoek	
"	14.7.16		One officer and eighteen men of the unit returned to Headquarters	
"	15.7.16		General duties, weather fine.	
"	16.7.16		General duties.	

Army Form C. 2118.

Instructions regarding War Diaries and Intelligence Summaries are contained in F. S. Regs., Part II. and the Staff Manual respectively. Title pages will be prepared in manuscript.

WAR DIARY
or
INTELLIGENCE SUMMARY.
(Erase heading not required.)

Place	Date	Hour	Summary of Events and Information	Remarks and references to Appendices
Sheet 2.8 S.9.d.6.0	16.7.16		Aid Posts & dumps rations received.	
"	17.7.16		General routine.	
"	18.7.16		Advance party of 1 Officer & one other rank relief Off 62nd F.A. & late run A.D.S & D.S.	
"	19.7.16		All out evacuated from F.A. hospital	
"	20.7.16		Two Officers & one section handed to FLETRE on advance party, A.D.S & D.S. handed over to 62nd F.A.	
"	21.7.16		Remainder of unit moved to FLETRE, arrived at 1 P.M. at the Château at FLETRE	
			transport moved to billets apart from 73 Brigade.	
"	22.7.16		All wagons park & section shifts to return town standartsie	
			Short front, general routine.	
FLETRE	22.7.16		Left FLETRE at 6.15 transferred to GODERSVELDE Station entrained V eyp at 11.45 p.m	
"	24.7.16		arriving at SALEUX at 9.15 detrain transferred to MOLLIENS-VIDAME at 5 A.M. weather fine	
MOLLIENS- VIDAME	25.7.16		Arrangements to billet and from 73 Brigade.	
"	26.7.16		General routine, weather fine	
"	27.7.16		General routine, weather fine	
"	28.7.16		General routine, weather fine very hot.	
"	29.7.16		General routine.	

Army Form C. 2118.

WAR DIARY
or
INTELLIGENCE SUMMARY.

(Erase heading not required.)

Instructions regarding War Diaries and Intelligence Summaries are contained in F. S. Regs., Part II. and the Staff Manual respectively. Title pages will be prepared in manuscript.

Place	Date	Hour	Summary of Events and Information	Remarks and references to Appendices
Sheet 19 A.L MULLENS V. DAME	30.7.16		Chind panels. Orders received at 6 P.M. for transfer to Transvl by road to Shef 62D/24 Bechel	
" "	31.7.16		Orders for remainder of unit to Transvl by road to HANGEST Thence by rail to VECQUEMONT. To march from there on following leaves webberwer to SALLY-LE-SEC + East thence to K4d21Shu16LD	

W.J.Maughan
Lt Colonel
O.C 73rd F.A.

August 1916.

24th Div.

93rd Field Ambulance.

51

Headquarters
Q Bch. 24th Division.

Herewith Original Copy of War Diary for August 1916.
Please acknowledge receipt.

[signature]
Lt Col
R.A.M.C.
OFFICER COMMANDING
73rd FIELD AMB. 24TH DIVISION.

R/86
31·8·16.

Ack'd
GWT.

Army Form C. 2118.

Vol 12

WAR DIARY
or
INTELLIGENCE SUMMARY

(Erase heading not required.)

Place	Date	Hour	Summary of Events and Information	Remarks and references to Appendices
Stat f & D O.S Chateau CORBIE	1.8.16		Orders received for Unit drawn of the unit to take over XIII Corps Rest Station at Chateau CORBIE. Left K14.A.2.1 at 9 a.m. arrived our Rest Station from 97.7A at noon. Number of ant latrines & offices 3 P.S. attn a.l. the Rest house 74.7.A	
"	2.8.16		form the remainder of the unit of Rest Station	
"	3.8.16		Party of 2 Officers & neighbours O.R. detailed for duty with 45 C.C.S	
"	4.8.16		Sick, average admitted to Rest Station 140.	
"	5.8.16		General routine, weather fine, very warm	
"	6.8.16		General routine	
"	7.8.16		General routine, no great actual to notice three hundred, thick parade.	
"	8.8.16		General routine, weather cooler	
"	9.8.16		General routine	
"	10.8.16		General routine, some rain	
"	11.8.16		General routine, some acid showers during evening	
"	12.8.16		General routine	
"	13.8.16		General routine	
"	14.8.16		One officer and 60 other ranks reported, one orgy killed all of the Bean division.	

WAR DIARY
INTELLIGENCE SUMMARY

Army Form C. 2118

(Erase heading not required.)

Place	Date	Hour	Summary of Events and Information	Remarks and references to Appendices
Shute 62 D C.5 Chateau CORBIE	15.8.16		Sir Rene Reinforcement reported for duty with Bearer division.	
"	16.8.16		Lieut STEWART joined Bearer division in place of Lieut KNIGHT wounded.	
"	17.8.16		CAPTAIN BRISCOE attached to D.M.T. A as reserve officer.	
"	18.8.16		Four other ranks wounded in Bearer division	
"	19.8.16		One N.C.O. & two privates killed & three wounded	
"	20.8.16		General routine, a considerable number of Bearers came into the with dysentery symptoms	
"	21.8.16		General routine	
"	22.8.16		General routine	
"	23.8.16		General routine	
"	24.8.16		General routine	
"	"		with some showers ; weather colder	
"	25.8.16		Lt. P.B. HARRISON reported for duty. Taken on strength.	
"	26.8.16		General routine and orders received to move on following day.	
"	27.8.16		Handed over XIV Corps Rest Station to O.C. 13th Field Ambulance and 7 cases handed over. 9 Officers	
"	"		and 243 other ranks, unit proceeded to D.3 0.6.3.7. & joined Bearer subdivn.	
D.30.63.7	28.8.16		Arrangements made to collect unit from 73 Brigade.	

Army Form C. 2118.

WAR DIARY
or
INTELLIGENCE SUMMARY.
(Erase heading not required.)

Instructions regarding War Diaries and Intelligence Summaries are contained in F. S. Regs., Part II. and the Staff Manual respectively. Title pages will be prepared in manuscript.

Place	Date	Hour	Summary of Events and Information	Remarks and references to Appendices
Sheet 62 D				
D.30.b.3.9.	29.8.16		One tent subdivision has transport detailed for duty with XV Corps Main Dressing Station, advance received for arrival 8th Oct. one nco. & 4 orderlies wounded post from 43rd F.A. in following day.	
" "	30.8.16		Point left tephounded & F.Y.D.9.9. I took over collecting post, weather very wet all day.	
" "	31.8.16		Party of 2 NCOs and their have been detailed to report (probably) with 72nd F.A. General reconnoitring cont. weather dry.	

W. G. Mayhew
Lt Colonel

PARIS
OFFICER COMMANDING
79th FIELD AMB. ...TH DIVISION.

140/734

24th Divn.

13rd Field Ambulance

COMMITTEE FOR THE
MEDICAL HISTORY OF THE WAR
Date 30 OCT. 1915

To
Headquarters
    Q Branch 24th Division

Herewith Original Copy of War Diary
for Sept 1916.

Please acknowledge receipt.

done J.L.W.

[signature]

Lt Col   R.A.M.C.
OFFICER COMMANDING
73rd FIELD AMB., 24th DIVISION.

[Stamp: 24th DIVISION / No. 2/5 / Date 30.9.16 / 73rd FIELD AMBULANCE, R.A.M.C.]

WAR DIARY
or
INTELLIGENCE SUMMARY

Army Form C. 2118.

Place	Date	Hour	Summary of Events and Information	Remarks and references to Appendices
Shelf 62D Fr.d.A.A.	1.9.16		General routine, very few walking wounded, weather fine.	
"	2.9.16		Party of 1 NCO and 40 OR from heavy batteries detailed to report for duty to OC 72 FA. Sergt Major RIGBY transferred to 23 FA for duty.	
"	3.9.16		General routine, very few walking wounded admitted during day 259	
"	4.9.16		General routine, three men Privates WRIGHT, KERR, AIREY wounded	
"	5.9.16		Movement order received & had our Divisional Collecting Post moved on to 2/5 West Lancs FA. left in D30.62.7 about 6PM. arrived about 5.30 p.m. all tents pitched in field, weather very wet, colour round A row by Road Bordenne, harnessed by road.	
LENS 11 BOUCHON	6.9.16		Reveille 3 a.m., all tents struck & harnessed up and left for unloading siding, entrained at 6 a.m. arrived at LONGPRE about 11 a.m., LM LONGPRE and marched to BOUCHON, billets obtained for all men, transport left D30.62.7 at LM 62.D at 9 A.M., weather fine	
"	"		Horsed fatigue, horsed arrived at BOUCHON at 4.30 P.M., all wagon unloaded & billet found	
"	7.9.16			
"	"		General routine, hot infection with collected from 73rd Inf. Brigade, weather fine	
"	8.9.16		General routine, weather fine, checking medical & surgical equipment.	
"	10.9.16		General routine, Church Parade.	

WAR DIARY or INTELLIGENCE SUMMARY

Army Form C. 2118.

Place	Date	Hour	Summary of Events and Information	Remarks and references to Appendices
Reserve LENS. II BOUCHON	11.9.16		General routine. Coy A.S.C. MT reinforcements reported. Lent ambulance from train drivers; stretcher repaint unit.	
"	12.9.16		General routine, weather fine	
"	13.9.16		General routine, route march, camp visited by G.O.C. division, slight shower, fine	
"	14.9.16		Reinforcement of seven privates joined transport unit, weather fine	
"	15.9.16		Unit of A.D.M.S. & one N.C.O. (Sergt) joined unit	
"	16.9.16		Orders received to be ready to move at short notice	
"	17.9.16		General routine. Church parade. Weather fine.	
"	18.9.16		Movement orders received. Walk-over. Very wet	
"	19.9.16		General routine. Ad. bdn. struck. 7.A. left for LONGPRE station & entrained at north transport landed on to 24th Suffolks Column.	
Ref 36B D25.a.24	20.9.16		Unit arrived by train at FOUQUEREUIL & detrained at 9 am and marched to MARLES-LES-MINES all men billeted in the village. Some motors reported for duty from 30th Suffs column.	
MARLES-LES-MINES	21.9.16		Unit left MARLES-LES-MINES at 10 am & marched with 73rd Inf. Brigade to HOUDAIN billets obtained for detachment, weather fine.	
"	22.9.16		Advance party of 6 officers and that party proceeded to GRAND SERVINS & took over advanced drawing station from 29 7A at ABLAIN ST. NAZAIRE X.10.6.32 & MOUNT ST ELOY T.8.a.34 with party of 50 men sent in advance to GRAND SERVINS.	
"	23.9.16		Remainder forced marched off at 7am & reached GRAND SERVINS at 10am. Weather fine. The unit relieved 29 7.A.	
GRAND SERVINS	24.9.16		General routine, all wounds redressed. No casualties, further transport reported also bus, motor cycles.	
"	25.9.16		General routine. Camp rearranged in own minor details	
"	26.9.16		General routine. Camp rearranged in own minor details	
"	27.9.16		19 O.R. left for 1st Army rest camp. F.A. relieved Y.30.C & 87th S Division	

WAR DIARY
or
INTELLIGENCE SUMMARY

Army Form C. 2118.

Place	Date	Hour	Summary of Events and Information	Remarks and references to Appendices
Reference Sheet 36.B GRAND SERVINS	28.9.16		General routine; general fatigues; new hutting made through camp. Shelter trench.	
"	29.9.16		General routine. Camp inspected by A.D.M.S. III Corps.	
"	30.9.16		General routine. Camp inspected by A.D.M.S. also inspected A.D.S at ABLAIN ST NAZAIRE.	

W. G. Maydon
Lt Colonel
O C 73rd Field Ambulance

140/18/4

Oct. 1916

24th Div.

73rd Field Ambulance.

COMMITTEE FOR THE
MEDICAL HISTORY OF THE WAR
Date -9 DEC. 1916

WAR DIARY or INTELLIGENCE SUMMARY

Army Form C. 2118.

24

Place	Date	Hour	Summary of Events and Information	Remarks and references to Appendices
P/S Sheet 36B @ 24 C6.9 GRAND SERAUMS	1.10.16		General routine. Church parade, weather fine.	
"	2.10.16		General duties & fatigue arrangements made for drawing comp, weather wet.	
"	3.10.16		General routine.	
"	4.10.16		General routine, weather very wet.	
"	5.10.16		General routine, eight men arrived as reinforcement later on the strength present.	
"	6.10.16		General routine, fatigue party & relaying duck boards, weather improving.	
"	7.10.16		General routine, a working party of 1 NCO & 14 O.R. detailed for duty in 'LE FOREST DE NIEPPE'	
"	8.10.16		General routine, weather stormy.	
"	9.10.16		General routine, weather fine.	
"	10.10.16		General routine, work of improving camp progressing.	
"	11.10.16		General routine, weather wet & stormy.	
"	12.10.16		General routine, relief sent to A.D.S. at ARLAIN ST. NAZAIRE; 1st Cdn of thereof awarded Military medal.	
"	13.10.16		General routine.	
"	14.10.16		General routine, weather very stormy, some snowstorms.	
"	15.10.16		Church parade.	
"	16.10.16		General routine. Lieut Stewart relieved Capt Redden as A.D.S. ABLAIN ST NAZAIRE	
"	17.10.16		General routine. one A.S.C. M.O. reported for duty. Weather fine	
"	18.10.16		General routine. One N.C.O. A.S.C. M.T. reported for duty. Weather cold	
"	19.10.16		General routine, routine.	
"	20.10.16		General routine.	

WAR DIARY
or
INTELLIGENCE SUMMARY

Army Form C. 2118.

Place	Date	Hour	Summary of Events and Information	Remarks and references to Appendices
G34 central Sheet 36B GRAND SERVINS	22/10/16		General Routine. One man to S.C.M.T. Transferred to 3rd Div Supply Column. Church Parade. Weather fair. Operation Orders received ADMS 24th Div re/ this Div taking over present 40th Div area.	
"	23/10/16		General Routine. Weather very wet.	
"	24/10/16		General Routine. Weather very wet.	
"	25/10/16		General routine. Weather wet & stormy, strong wind.	
"	26/10/16		General fatigues. Detachment from Buffs School of Instruction reported to Headquarters.	
"	27/10/16		General routine. (T.W.74 F.A.) 8/22 O.R. reported for temporary duty & proceeded to relieve (T.W.74 F.A.) 8/22 O.R. Sheet 36.c advance party of 2.N.C.D. & further men ONT of BRACQUEMONT A.D.S at G35.d.3.7 Sheet 36.c. advance party of 2.N.C.D. & further men out at BRACQUEMONT A.D.S. at MOUNT ST ELOY & ABLAIN ST. NAZAIRE later on advance parties from No.1 CANADIAN F.A. Personnel returned to F.A. Headquarters	
"	28/10/16		Working parties from front of NIEPPE returned to Headquarters. Headed on evening return at GRAND SERVINS & No.1 CANADIAN F.A. no green lead cave 73 rich cent left travelled to BRAQUEMONT L25 61.3 all men billeted in huts. Weather very wet. G25.d.3.7 and G22.c.6.6	
Sheet 36B Y 26 C	29/10/16		Got an ADS started at G.20.a.3.0, G.25.d.3.7 136 F.A. the no of oct 2 officer	
"	30/10/16		Took over alterations & dressing station from 136 F.A. the no of oct 2 officer & 44 O.R. weather still very wet & stormy.	
"	31/10/16		General fatigues encamping moved dressing station.	

[signature] J.G. Snyder
R.A.M.C.
OFFICER COMMANDING
FIELD AMB — DIVISION

140/265

24th Div.

73rd Field Ambulance

Nov 1915

COMMITTEE FOR THE
MEDICAL HISTORY OF THE WAR
Date -3 JAN. 1917

Army Form C. 2118.

73ᵈ F.A.

Nov /15

WAR DIARY
or
INTELLIGENCE SUMMARY

(Erase heading not required.)

Instructions regarding War Diaries and Intelligence Summaries are contained in F.S. Regs., Part II. and the Staff Manual respectively. Title Pages will be prepared in manuscript.

Place	Date	Hour	Summary of Events and Information	Remarks and references to Appendices
Sht 36 B L.25.6.3 BRAQUEMONT	1.11.16		General fatigues, removing of dining station, weather cold & stormy, some rain.	
"	2.11.16		Dining station inspected by D.D.M.S. 1st Corps, general routine, weather very wet.	
"	3.11.16		General routine, weather wet & stormy. The number of wounded admitted few.	
"	4.11.16		General routine, fatigues.	
"	5.11.16		General routine.	
"	6.11.16		Health still strong, tent members in addition work very difficult.	
"	7.11.16		General routine, weather very wet, undertaking 1st Division about in 24 hours an all cases evacuated through A.D.S., G.P. and & J.A. of 6th Division.	
"	8.11.16		General routine, continued wet weather.	
"	9.11.16		T.O.C. of Division visit A.D.M.S. inspected Field Ambulance.	
"	10.11.16		General routine, weather fair.	
"	11.11.16		General routine, visit of A.D.S. formerly acts frosty.	
"	12.11.16		General routine, thank harvest.	
"	13.11.16		General routine, men of the unit visited in use of new bomb contains M.E. Tent	
"	14.11.16		General routine in tent town of St. GEORGE'S A.D.S. advised, general routine.	
"	15.11.16		General routine.	
"	16.11.16		General routine, from O.R. rents arrived station on the strength.	
"	17.11.16		General routine, laying more men entitled, weather very cold some snow.	
"	18.11.16		Health not, much colder weather. Sticking of page	
"	19.11.16		Inspection of Unit by Gd Army Commander, weather wet.	

Army Form C. 2118.

WAR DIARY
or
INTELLIGENCE SUMMARY

(Erase heading not required.)

Instructions regarding War Diaries and Intelligence Summaries are contained in F. S. Regs., Part II. and the Staff Manual respectively. Title Pages will be prepared in manuscript.

Place	Date	Hour	Summary of Events and Information	Remarks and references to Appendices
Sheet 36/B L25.6.3 BRAQUEMONT	20.11.16		General routine.	
"	21.11.16		General orders, weather fine.	
"	22.11.16		General duties. Lieut A.S.C. reinforcements reported for duty.	
"	23.11.16		General routine.	
"	24.11.16		General routine, work of repairs; A.D.S. prevailing extending, weather fine.	
"	25.11.16		General routine, very wet.	
"	26.11.16		Church parade, weather fine.	
"	27.11.16		General routine, weather fine.	
"	28.11.16		General routine.	
"	29.11.16		General routine.	
"	30.11.16		General routine.	

W. G. Maydon
Lt Colonel
O.C. 13th 7 A

140/90=

24th Dev

13rd Field Ambulance

COMMITTEE FOR THE
MEDICAL HISTORY OF THE WAR
Date 31 JAN. 1917

T332

Army Form C. 2118.

WAR DIARY
or
INTELLIGENCE SUMMARY

(Erase heading not required.)

73 3rd Amb

Vol 16

Instructions regarding War Diaries and Intelligence Summaries are contained in F. S. Regs., Part II. and the Staff Manual respectively. Title Pages will be prepared in manuscript.

Place	Date	Hour	Summary of Events and Information	Remarks and references to Appendices
Sheet 36 B L25.6.2.5	1.12.16		General routine.	
"	2.12.16		Party of men at A.D.S. Loos relieved the party consisted 1 NCO and eleven men, weather fine	
"	3.12.16		Church parade, general routine	
"	4.12.16		General routine, weather fine.	
"	5.12.16		General routine, filling of ruts and sweeping of gutters round establishments	
"	6.12.16		General routine.	
"	7.12.16		General routine, weather fine.	
"	8.12.16		General routine, weather very wet.	
"	9.12.16		General routine, weather very wet.	
"	10.12.16		General routine.	
"	11.12.16		General routine, weather fine & bright.	
"	12.12.16		General routine, weather again very wet.	
"	13.12.16		General routine, inspected unit by A.O.C. division.	
"	14.12.16		General routine, three instruments refitted for duty.	
"	15.12.16		General routine, weather fine. Headquarters of Field Ambulance inspected by A.O.C. 1st brigade and A.O.C. division	
"	16.12.16		General routine, weather fine.	
"	17.12.16		Church parade.	
"	18.12.16		General routine	
"	19.12.16		General routine, weather fine.	
"	20.12.16		General routine.	
"	21.12.16		General routine, weather wet & stormy.	

Army Form C. 2118.

WAR DIARY
or
INTELLIGENCE SUMMARY

(Erase heading not required.)

Instructions regarding War Diaries and Intelligence Summaries are contained in F. S. Regs., Part II. and the Staff Manual respectively. Title Pages will be prepared in manuscript.

Place	Date	Hour	Summary of Events and Information	Remarks and references to Appendices
Sheet 36/13 L25.625	22.12.16		General routine.	
" "	23.12.16		General routine; weather very strong.	
" "	24.12.16		General routine; thank field.	
" "	25.12.16		General routine; divine service, also personnel at Headquarters F.A.	
" "	26.12.16		General routine; weather fine.	
" "	27.12.16		Half of personnel at A.D.S. St GEORGE and PHILOSOPHE relieved	
" "	28.12.16		Remainder of personnel relieved at A.D.S. weather very wet.	
" "	29.12.16		General routine; weather very wet.	
" "	30.12.16		General routine; weather fine, rookies led for clean.	
" "	31.12.16		General routine; thank parade.	

W. G. Greyson
Col
O.C. 78th Field Ambulance

140/1943

24th Div.

43rd. Field Ambulance

COMMITTEE FOR THE
MEDICAL HISTORY OF THE WAR
Date 13 MAR. 1917

WAR DIARY
or
INTELLIGENCE SUMMARY

Army Form C. 2118.

73 3rd Aust
Vol 17

Place	Date	Hour	Summary of Events and Information	Remarks and references to Appendices
Shed 36B L25, 61.3	1.1.17		General routine; stood down for sick also tonsured for this able to attend. Weather fine.	
BRACQUEMONT	2.1.17		General routine; weather mild	
"	3.1.17		General routine; Captain Bruce relieved Captain PLAYFAIR at A.D.S. ST. PATRICK, LOOS.	
"	4.1.17		General routine;	
"	5.1.17		General routine; Relief of men from 94th F.A. sent to A.D.S. ST PATRICK G35.d.3.7 Shed 36C	
"	6.1.17		General routine; Captain G.W.R. RUDKIN & Capt Major J.B. NEWTON returned in Dufokers	
"	7.1.17		General routine; Church Parade, weather mild.	
"	8.1.17		Pats of entire been consisting of his NCOs and twelve men sent on extra leave to A.D.S Shed 36C	
"	9.1.17		General routine; weather mild.	R. GEORGES G23.6.6.8
"	10.1.17		General routine; GERMAN wounded from attack at G.	
"	11.1.17		General routine; snow storm;	
"	12.1.17		General routine; two returned B.O.R. reported, weather strong	
"	13.1.17		General routine;	G 23.5.d.3.7. & most mr sensual
"	14.1.17		Entire from out to A.D.S at G 23.6.6.9 (vf Shed 36C) and to G 35.d.3.7 & most no unwell	
"	15.1.17		Out by 1st Mob. Royal Fusiliers. Thirteen wounded cases and eight and one wounded GERMAN elwelled, on men of the went wounded slightly	
"	16.1.17		General routine; all return have returned to F.A. Headquarters.	
"	17.1.17		General routine; weather cold strong;	
"	18.1.17		One NCO & twelve men sent as relief to A.D.S at G23.6.8.	
"	19.1.17		General routine; weather cold strong	
"	20.1.17		General routine; weather fine	
"	21.1.17		Handed over command of unit to Captain J.W.M. CUNNINGHAM R.A.M.C. M Maydonnell 1073 F.A.

Army Form C. 2118.

WAR DIARY
13th Field Ambulance
INTELLIGENCE SUMMARY

January 1914 Page 2

(Erase heading not required.)

Instructions regarding War Diaries and Intelligence Summaries are contained in F. S. Regs., Part II. and the Staff Manual respectively. Title Pages will be prepared in manuscript.

Place	Date	Hour	Summary of Events and Information	Remarks and references to Appendices
BRAQUEMONT	21-1-17		Captain F.W.M. CUNNINGHAM R.A.M.C. assumed command of 13th Field Ambulance at Braquemont.	Capt. Rew
"	22-1-17	12 noon	today vice Lt. Col. Hayden R.A.M.C. proceeding to England. General routine at unit H.Q. two wounded Germans admitted to this unit	JMM
"	23-1-17		General routine. 3 men from St. Georges A.D.S. went on leave and were relieved from Hosp. Capt. D.H. PAUL R.A.M.C. reported for temporary duty and was attached for instruction.	JMM
"	24-1-17		General Routine. Capt. WEIGALL R.A.M.C. on discharge from hospital was sent to H.Q. 2 N.C.O.s and 14 men for emergencies both to H.Q. unit for duty. Received secret instructions of an intended Raid to be sent at from H.Q. 2 N.C.O.s and 14 men for emergencies to PHILOSOPHE A.D.S.	JMM
"	25-1-17		General Routine. The Raid took place at 12 noon. It was by Canadians so the known were not required. Got confidential notice from A.D.M.S. that another raid on a large scale was expected tomorrow at dawn to gave order that the whole men to be kept at A.D.S. and detailed Captain BEAVEN and Lieut. CRIMP to assist at A.D.S.	JMM

PLAYFAIR in charge of

13 Field Ambulance   January 1914   Army Form C. 2118

WAR DIARY or INTELLIGENCE SUMMARY

Page III

Place	Date	Hour	Summary of Events and Information	Remarks and references to Appendices
BRAQUEMONT	26-1-19		General routine. A successful raid took place at daylight - Very few British wounded - 1 German wounded prisoner came to this unit. The party of extra bearers all returned to H.Q in the evening. Received orders about the move into rest area at BOMY.	JHM
BRAQUEMONT	27-1-19		General routine. Visited Brigade H.Q. to arrange about the men & medical arrangements for the March - Jade in the evening heard that the move was cancelled -	JHM
"	28-1-17		Arranged billets for the Hars of A.D.S at St Patricks and Philosophe. Also for 11 O.Rs at Philosophe. Visited Philosophe St PATRICKS and Mo posts of the Sussex R. Fusiliers and Stenwork.	JHM
"	29-1-19		Capt. Rayson + Lieut. Crump relieved Capt. Briscoe and Capt. Rudkin respectively at St. PATRICKS and PHILOSOPHE A.D.S. Visited A.T.S. at St. GEORGES and MO post of W. KENT Regiment. Also HALF WAY House	JHM

1875 Wt. W593/826 1,000,000 4/15 J.B.C. & A. A.D.S.S./Forms/C. 2118.

Army Form C. 2118

73. Field Ambulance WAR DIARY or INTELLIGENCE SUMMARY

January 1919 Page 4

(Erase heading not required.)

Instructions regarding War Diaries and Intelligence Summaries are contained in F. S. Regs., Part II. and the Staff Manual respectively. Title Pages will be prepared in manuscript.

Place	Date	Hour	Summary of Events and Information	Remarks and references to Appendices
BRAQUEMONT	30-1-19		General Routine. Nothing of importance to note.	
	31-1-19		Accompanied the A.D.M.S. round part of the front area — Visited the R.A.M.C. Post at CHALK PITS, A.D.S. at St. PATRICKS, Aid Posts of the Middlesex Stewards and Buffs also the Soup Kitchen of the Stewards. Otherwise usual routine and nothing of importance to note.	

J.H.Cunningham
Capt. R.A.M.C.
O.C. 73rd Field Ambulance

140/1921

24th Div.

73rd Field Ambulance

Feb. 1917

COMMITTEE FOR THE
MEDICAL HISTORY OF THE W.
Date 4.—APR.1917

Army Form C. 2118

WAR DIARY
or
INTELLIGENCE SUMMARY

(Erase heading not required.)

43rd Field Ambulance

February 1919

Page 1

Place	Date	Hour	Summary of Events and Information	Remarks and references to Appendices
BRAQUEMONT	1-2-19		General Routine – The weather remains very cold + hard frost –	Diagrammatic Evacuation Scheme of 43rd F.A.
"	2-2-19		General Routine – The A.D.M.S. 1st Corps inspected the hospital in the afternoon. Proceeded to A.D.S. at PHILOSOPHE and recommended several alterations in specially in the post house and sanitary arrangements which have been taken in hand. Two O.R. proceeded on leave.	
"	3-2-19		General Routine – Capt. Brisset returns Capt. Maughman at St GEORGE'S A.D.S. – Capt. Bain was detailed for permanent duty with 8th Buffs.	
"	4-2-19		General Routine – Capt. Baldwin proceeds to St PATRICK'S in relief of Capt. Playfair who is being evacuated sick. Capt. Weigall and 4 O.R. proceeded on leave –	
"	5-2-19		General routine – Captain Brown on relief by Capt Moclarty (returned from special leave to Canada) M.O. of 8 R.W. Kent Reg. reports for duty with H.Q. 43rd F.A. Captain Playfair evacuated to C.C.S.	

43rd Field Ambulance WAR DIARY or INTELLIGENCE SUMMARY

Army Form C. 2118

February 1917 Page 11

Place	Date	Hour	Summary of Events and Information	Remarks and references to Appendices
BRAQUEMONT	6-2-17		General Routine - Capt. Brown and Lieut. Crump posted to this unit and taken on permanent strength - visits ADSs at PHILOSOPHE and ST. GEORGES also R.A.M.C. Post at HALF WAY HOUSE. Suggests various sanitary & cooking improvements - Corpl. Latham left for England to take up a commission + was struck off the strength.	
"	7-2-17		Accompanies D.D.M.S. 1st Corps round the advanced dressing stations - Lieut. O'Farrell proceeds light permanent duty with 9th Reserve Park & was struck off the strength - Lieut. A. E. Brice reports for duty and was taken on the strength -	
"	8-2-17		General Routine - 2 horse transport left for England to take up a commission - Capt. Brown relieved Capt. Ruskin at St. Patrick -	
"	9-2-17		General Routine. O.C. 48th F.A. visits this ambulance & Philosophe with a view of taking over in near future - Capt. Brice of 74th F.A. reports for duty at St. George vice Capt. Ruskin sick -	

43rd Field Ambulance WAR DIARY / INTELLIGENCE SUMMARY
February 1917 — Page III

Place	Date	Hour	Summary of Events and Information	Remarks and references to Appendices
BRAQUEMONT	10-2-17		General routine. Short orders received for transport of Unit to ANNEZIN on 13/2/17. Staff arrangements for Ambulance transport to accompany 43rd Infantry Brigade on the March. Also operation orders for relief. Advance party of 2 officers + 50 men from 48th F.A. to take over O.S.'s and wounded German Prisoners admitted who died shortly afterwards. JRM	Orders attached.
	11-2-17		General routine. Made arrangements to entrain Braun in view of expected snow storm. Snow operations common to all officers. JRM	
	12-2-17		All O.B.'s taken over by 48th F.A. All officers + men returned to H.Q. Consolidation of move to ANNEZIN received but no notification yet of when we are to go to. JRM	
NOEUX-les-MINES	13-2-17		43rd F.A. handed over to 48th F.A. All F.A. site at BRAQUEMONT 2 p.m. The 43rd F.A. moved to NOEUX-les-MINES where they remained cleaning — Billets by Sections — Billets very bad + draughty.	

139 Field Ambulance

WAR DIARY
or
INTELLIGENCE SUMMARY

Army Form C. 2118

February 1919
Page IV

Place	Date	Hour	Summary of Events and Information	Remarks and references to Appendices
Noeux-les-MINES	14-2-19		General Routine according to attached Programme. The small town opened as Inspection room - Including the sick from ANNEZIN FOUQUERES and NOEUX	Programmes of training attached. JKM
	15-2-19		LES MINES and evacuations from Immediately to 48 C.C.S. General Routine according to attached Programme	JKM
	16-2-19		" " " " " Dr. Williamson wounded wife	JKM
	17-2-19		Stand to - "A" Section inoculated and all precautions taken. General Routine - Capt. Riddie wounded to E.C.S.	JKM
	18-2-19		General Routine according to Programme - Received orders about doctor & Infective virus cases and new arrangements accordingly direct with R.M.O's.	JKM
	19-2-19		General Routine according to programme -	JKM
	20-2-19		" " " " Captain Biden reports for duty from the	JKM
	21-2-19		Base & Lieut. Price received orders to join 104" Brigade RFA forthwith - General Routine - Capt. Wilson reports for duty vice Capt. Brown who took his place with 1st R.F.	JKM
	22-2-19		General Routine according to Programme	JKM

/13" Field Ambulance

WAR DIARY
or
INTELLIGENCE SUMMARY

Army Form C. 2118

February 1917

Place	Date	Hour	Summary of Events and Information	Remarks and references to Appendices
NOEUX-LES-MINES	23-2-19		General Routine according to Programme. Lt. Caird went on leave for 10 days.	First Year Programme attached.
	24-2-19		" " " " O.O. 125 Received from 11th I.B.	
	25-2-19		" " " "	
	26-2-19		" " " " Visits 50th F.A. at BRAQUEMONT	
	27-2-19		Went this unit is shortly to take over.	
	28-2-19		General Routine according to Programme.	Programme of doing attached.

J.B. Cunningham
Lt. U. Rann
O.C. 73 F.A.

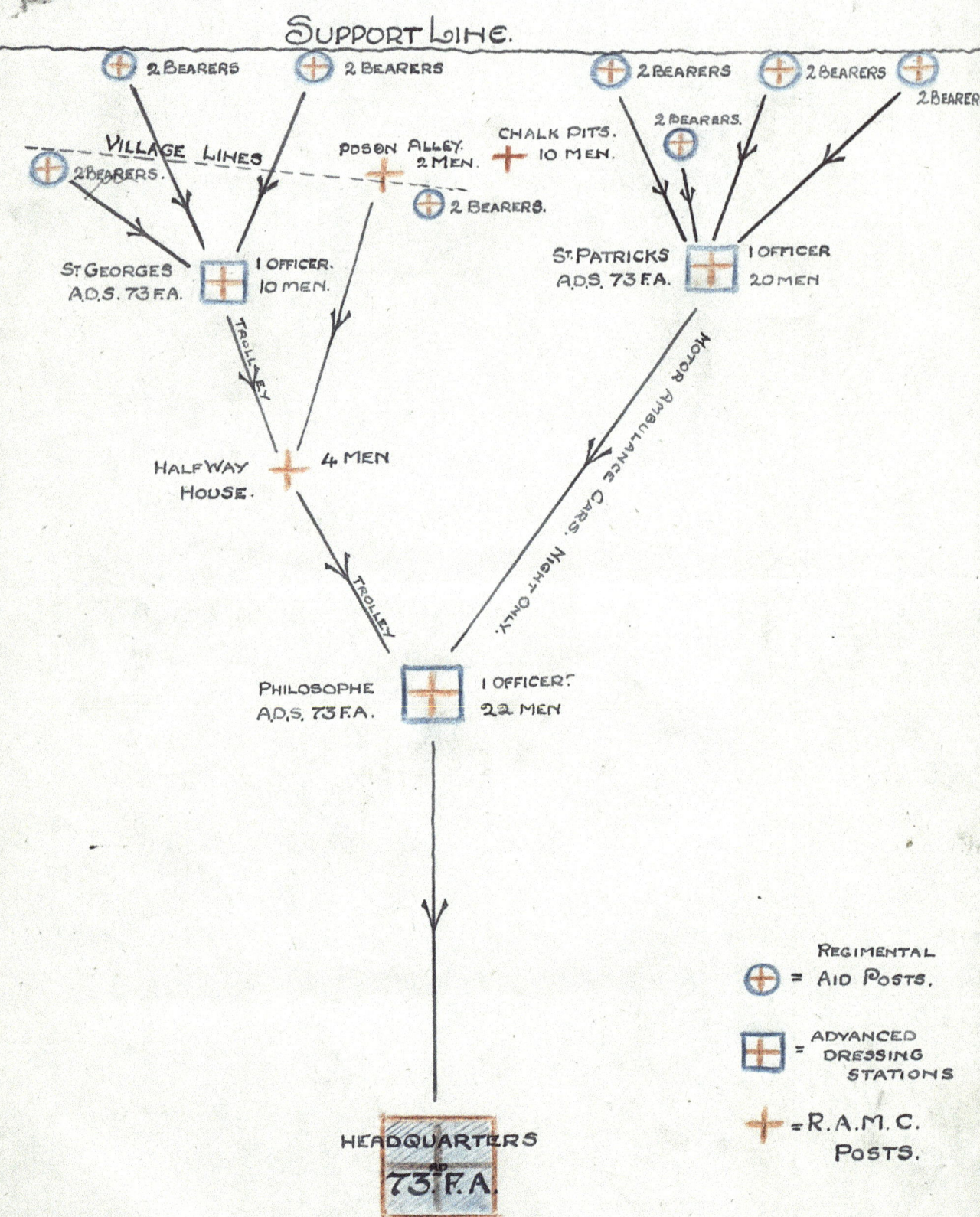

T. W. Pennington
Capt. R.A.M.C.
O.C. 73rd Fld. Ambce.

10.2.17

Copy No. (1.) File
" " (2.) Brig. Major. 73 I.B.
" " (3)(4.) War Diary
" " (5) O.C. 448th Fld. Amb.
" " (6-15) All Officers. 73 F.A.
" " (16) Sgt. Major.

1 SECRET   **73rd Field Ambulance.**

Movement Orders.   Copy No 14

Feby. 11th 1917.

      Two Horse Ambulances will report to the M.O. 13th Middlesex Regt. at the Square, BRAQUEMONT, at 9.15 A.M. for duty. They will return to Headquarters on completion of the march.

Advanced Dressing Stations.

      Three M.O.s and about 60 other ranks from 48th Field Ambulance will report during the course of the morning to the M.O. i/c PHILOSOPHE, who will provide guides, and arrange for their distribution at the 3 advanced dressing stations.

      On relief, personnel of 73rd Field Ambulance with the exception of one M.O., one N.C.O., and one man at each advanced dressing station, will assemble a PHILOSOPHE, and will proceed to headquarters unit at BRAQUEMONT.

      Ambulance cars after relief by the cars of incoming unit will immediately proceed to Headquarters & report arrival. The car orderlies will remain behind as guides to the incoming cars for 24 hours.

      The three M.O.s will assist the incoming unit in the collection & evacuation of sick & wounded on the night of the 11th-12th, and on completion will proceed independently to Headquarters

The 3 selected N.C.O's & men will help in addition on the night of the 12th-13th, & on completion will report at PHILOSOPHE before proceeding to headquarters.

French Stores, Ordnance Stores, Trench Maps, & Schemes of evacuation will be handed over to incoming unit. Only Mobilisation Medical Equipment & Wheeled Stretchers belonging to Unit will be brought away.

February 12th.

One horse ambulance will report to M.O. 2nd Leinsters Regt. at the Square, BRAQUEMONT, at 9.15 a.m.

One horse ambulance will report to M.O. 7th Northants Regt. at Cross Roads, PETIT SAINS, at 9.15 a.m. & on completion of duty, they will return to Headquarters.

Lieut. Price & 1 Motor Ambce will start from LES BREBIS at 11 a.m. & will follow the route taken by the 9th Royal Sussex Regt. earlier in the morning, to pick up any men who may have fallen out. After disposal of any such cases, he will return to headquarters.

February 13th

At 7 a.m. the advanced party of 48th Fd. Amb. will take over the Main Dressing Station at BRAQUEMONT, as arranged between O.C. 48th Fd. Amb. and O.C. 73rd Fd. Amb.

73rd Field Ambce will proceed to ANNEZIN on Fby. 13th at a time to be notified later.

Capt. Rudkin and an advanced party will proceed to ANNEZIN, numbers & time to be notified later.

73rd Field Ambulance.

Programme of Training in Rest Area.

Week Ending Sat. February 17th 1917.

Time.	Wednesday.	Thursday.	Friday.	Saturday.
6.45 A.M. to 7 A.M.	Reveille and Roll Call.	Do.	Do.	Do.
7.30 A.M. to 9.15 A.M.	Breakfast & Cleaning up etc.	Do.	Do.	Do.
9.15 A.M.	Section Officers Inspection Parade.	Do.	Do.	Do.
9.30 A.M. to 10.20 A.M.	General Routine	Section Drill & Red Ambce Drill.	Section Drill Stretcher Drill Red Ambce Drill.	Section Drill Red Ambce Drill.
10.30 A.M. to 12.15 p.m.	General Routine	Route March.	Do.	Route March.
12.30 p.m.	Dinner	Do.	Do.	Do.
2 p.m. to 4 p.m.	Football.	Football.	Football.	Route March.
9 p.m.	Roll Call	Do.	Do.	Do.
9.30 p.m.	"Lights Out".	Do.	Do.	Do.

NOTE.
1. "A" Section parades, drills, & route marches separately from Friday.
2. Bath Parade when available.
   Liable to alteration, by weather circumstances.

J.M. Cunningham
R.A.M.C.
OFFICER COMMANDING
73rd FIELD AMB. 7th DIVISION

73rd Field Ambulance. R.A.M.C.

Programme of Training in Rest Area.

Week Ending Saturday Feb. 24th '17.

Time.	Sunday	Monday	Tuesday	Wednesday	Thursday	Friday	Saturday
6.45am to 7am.	Reveille and Roll Call			Ditto			
7.30am to 9.15am.	Breakfast & Cleaning of Billets			Ditto			
9.15 am.	Divine Service	Section Officers' Inspection Parade		Ditto			
9.30am to 10.20 am.	Holy Communion	Section Drill.	Section Drill.	Gas Helmet Drill.	Section Drill.	Physical and Section Drill.	Stretcher Drill.
10.30am to 12.15pm.	General Routine	Field Amb. and Physical Drill.	Route March	Physical and Section Drill.	Stretcher Drill	Field Amb. and Wagon Drill	Route March
12.30 pm.	Dinner.			Ditto			
2pm. to 4pm.	General Routine Special Service for "A" Section.	Football Match	Football Match	Route March	Football Match	Route March	Football Match
6 pm.	Roll Call						
9 pm.	Roll Call			Ditto			
9.30 pm.	"Lights Out"			Ditto			

February 17th 1917.

1. "A" Section Parades, drills, route marches etc. separately.
2. Bath Parades when baths available.
3. Health Inspection – Mondays. at 7.30 pm.
4. Liable to alteration by weather or circumstances.

Lieut. Col. R.A.M.C.
Officer Commanding
73rd Field Amb. ...th DIVISION

73rd Field Ambulance

Programme of Training in Rest Area.

Week ending Sat. March 3rd 1917.

Time	Sunday	Monday	Tuesday	Wednesday	Thursday	Friday	Saturday
6.45 a.m. to 7 a.m.	Reveille Roll Call	-Do-	-Do-	-Do-	-Do-	-Do-	-Do-
7.30 am to 9.15 am	Breakfast Cleaning up	-Do- Section Officers	-Do-	-Do-	-Do-	-Do-	-Do-
9.15 am	Divine Service Inspection Parade						
9.30 am to 10.30 am	Holy Communion	Section Drill Field Ambce	Field Ambce Section Drill	Section Drill	Gas Helmet Drill	Section Squad Drill	Section Drill
10.30 am to 12.15 pm	General Routine	Physical Drill	Parade at 10.30am with Skeleton order for 15 miles Route March	K.I. Inspection 2nd erecting of Inoculating Equipment	Section & Field Amber Wagon Drill	Field Ambce Wagon Drill	Route March
12.30 p.m.	Dinner	-Do-		Dinner	Dinner	-Do-	-Do-
2 pm to 4 pm	General Routine	Football		Route March	Football Match	Route Football March	
6 p.m.	Special Service for "A" Section						
9.30 p.m.	Lights Out	-Do-	-Do-	-Do-	-Do-	-Do-	-Do-

NOTE 1. "A" Section parades, mills, route marches separately. 2. Bath parade when available. Health inspection - Mondays 1.30 p.m.
Liable to alteration by weather circumstances.

Feby. 24th 1917

Lieut. Col. R.A.M.C.
Officer Commanding
73rd Field Amb. th Division

140/2042

Nov 1917

24th Div.

73rd Field Ambulance

COMMITTEE FOR THE
MEDICAL HISTORY OF THE WAR
Date 11 MAY. 1917

WAR DIARY or INTELLIGENCE SUMMARY

Army Form C. 2118

"/3" Field Ambulance

March 1919

Page —1

Place	Date	Hour	Summary of Events and Information	Remarks and references to Appendices
NOEUX-LES-MINES	1-3-19		General Routine – Issued operation order Part 1 –	Operation order Part 1 + 11 attached –
"	2-3-19		"B" Section left at 1:30 to relieve 3rd Canadian F.A. at A.D.S. BULLY GRENAY. POINT GRENAY and their respective R.A.M.C. post – Q.O.R. reinforcements reported.	
BRAQUEMONT	3-3-19		Advance party left at 4:30 to take over F.A. site from 50th F.A. L.26.6.3.4. Remainder left at 9:30 am the relief was complete by 12 noon. Took over 2 Officers + 4 O.R. patients.	
"	4-3-19		General Routine – Feeding of personnel + minor duties. Visits the R.A.P. A.D.S at BULLY GRENAY also R.A.M.C. Post in BOVRIL TRENCH and St GRENAY. Arranged of 1st R.Fusiliers and D.D.S at CALONNE and St GRENAY. Several changes as the use of the light Railway.	
"	5-3-19		General Routine – 2 A.S.C M.T. reports for duty.	
"	6-3-19		General Routine in organising the work of the unit – Lieut. Crump returned from leave – H.Q. of the unit inspected by A.D.M.S. of the Division – Working Party sent over to Girls School – the site of adjacent F.A.	

73rd Field Ambulance WAR DIARY

Army Form C. 2118

INTELLIGENCE SUMMARY

March 1919

Page 11

Place	Date	Hour	Summary of Events and Information	Remarks and references to Appendices
BRAQUEMONT	4-3-19		D.D.M.S. 1st Corps inspected the Field Ambulance. Visits O.C. 8th A.F.A. & posts during the afternoon & decided to try a more economical line of evacuation from the 9th. Sgt. Robertson A.S.C. M.T. transferred to 196 Coy. A.S.C. & replaced by Sgt. Ingram. General Routine. Notification received to H.Q.C.M. on Sgt. Walton + other witnesses wanted.	JMcL
"	8-3-19			JMcL
"	9-3-19		A.D.M.S. + D.A.D. 2nd Division visits all the A.D.S.'s and R.A.P.'s of this sector. Settles to make the post at CALONNE into an A.D.S. but this will take some time & permit system of evacuation has got forth present. Otherwise General Routine – nothing of importance to note.	JMcL JMcL
"	10-3-19			JMcL
"	11-3-19		Visits the A.D.S. + the O.C. 104 Coy R.E. to talk arrangements to the transport skills & m.... labour to make an A.D.S. at CALONNE.	JMcL

13th Field Ambulance WAR DIARY or INTELLIGENCE SUMMARY

Army Form C. 2118

March 1919

Page III

Place	Date	Hour	Summary of Events and Information	Remarks and references to Appendices
Braquemont	12-3-19		From today the 10th M.A.C. are to evacuate all infectious cases cup cases and leg injury wounds which are to be collected at 13. F.A. from this area - Made arrangements for the reception of infectious cases - to "C" section taking ½ "B" section of the A.D.S.	June
	13-3-19		The relief of "B" by "C" section was completed at A.D.S. Sergeant Walker returned to ranks by order of F.G.C.M. on 10th instant - June. Captain F.S. with the hospital.	June
	14-3-19		Usual Routine - A.D.M.S. visits the hospital.	
	15-3-19		General Routine - Captain Biden was transferred to 2nd Junction on R.M.O. + Lieut. Ranger returned for temporary duty in place -	
	16-3-19		General Routine - Nothing of importance to note -	
	17-3-19		Staff-Sergt. Art. proceeds to England to take up a commission - Pt. McWilla transferred to No 1. A.D.M.S. for duty - Batch of the smell of strength - B.O.R. temporarily reports for duty & taken on the strength - Vide A.D.S. at Burray Brenay. A.D.S.S./Forms/C.2118.

1/3rd Field Ambulance WAR DIARY March 1917 Army Form C. 2118
or
INTELLIGENCE SUMMARY

Page ...

Place	Date	Hour	Summary of Events and Information	Remarks and references to Appendices
BRAQUEMONT	18-3-17		Attend a meeting of ADMS and O.C. Field Ambulances of 1st Corps. Various questions re admin operations especially as regards evacuation of wounded both lying down and walking cases discussed.	J.J.M.
	19-3-17		General Routine – Nothing of note to record.	J.J.M.
	20-3-17		Pte. Proper transferred to No. 18 F.A. and Pte. Buck to 2/1st F.F.E. on strength of the strength. Visits the new A.D.S. at CALONNE which is making good progress & which seems to reduce by one – Stretcher to the tunnel from Stalls One to front line and arrange that the battery through this tunnel for evacuation – Captain Sproule reports return for duty as one walking constitution –	J.J.M.
	21-3-17			
	22-3-17		A.D.M.S. visits this unit – Arranged to a Sanitary scheme at station in want of attention etc. Visits Bully GRENAY, Pt GRENAY and R.A.P. of Life (?) direct from there.	J.J.M.

73rd Field Ambulance

Army Form C. 2118

WAR DIARY or INTELLIGENCE SUMMARY

March 1917 — Page V

(Erase heading not required.)

Place	Date	Hour	Summary of Events and Information	Remarks and references to Appendices
BRAQUEMONT	23-3-17		General Routine — Nothing of importance to note —	
"	24-3-17		Main Dressing Station inspected by A.D.M.S. 24th Division — Visits A.D.S. at Bully Grenay + Colonne — The work of the latter place is progressing well — The Relief of "C" Section by "B" Section in front area commenced today — 1 Officer + 14 O.R. exchanging — Same time commenced tonight. 11 p.m. Resumed. 12 midnight.	
"	25-3-17		General Routine — Still of importance to note.	53rd
"	26-3-17		A.D.M.S. 14th Divn. inspected Unit — Visits Calonne + Bully Grenay — The method of evacuation is two cheery lorries, sea attached diagrammatic scheme, but the use of labour has capable of taking 18 lying cases will not be available until the arrangements in the trench are completed — The Stride wounded sick and struck off the Roll strength. The Relief of "C" by "A" Section was completed today.	Diagrammatic Scheme of evacuation attached.
"	27-3-17		Visits A.D.S. with M.O. of M.S. 21st Division — spent a new Beau fort forging. 4 O.R. at St. Hoare —	

13th Field Ambulance WAR DIARY
INTELLIGENCE SUMMARY
March 1919
Army Form C. 2118
Page VI

Place	Date	Hour	Summary of Events and Information	Remarks and references to Appendices
BRAQUEMONT	28-3-19		General Routine. Captain Sproule returned to 13 M.A.C.	Ystrad
"	29-3-19		General Routine. Nil of importance to note.	Ystrad
"	30-3-19		S.B.M.S. visits this unit - Offence nil of importance to note.	Ystrad
"	31-3-19		A.D.M.S. visits this unit. Received orders to detail 2 N.C.Os + 8 privates to proceed to No 33 P.C.S. when required for temporary duty.	Ystrad

J.H. Cunningham Lieut.
D.A.
O.C. 13. F.A.

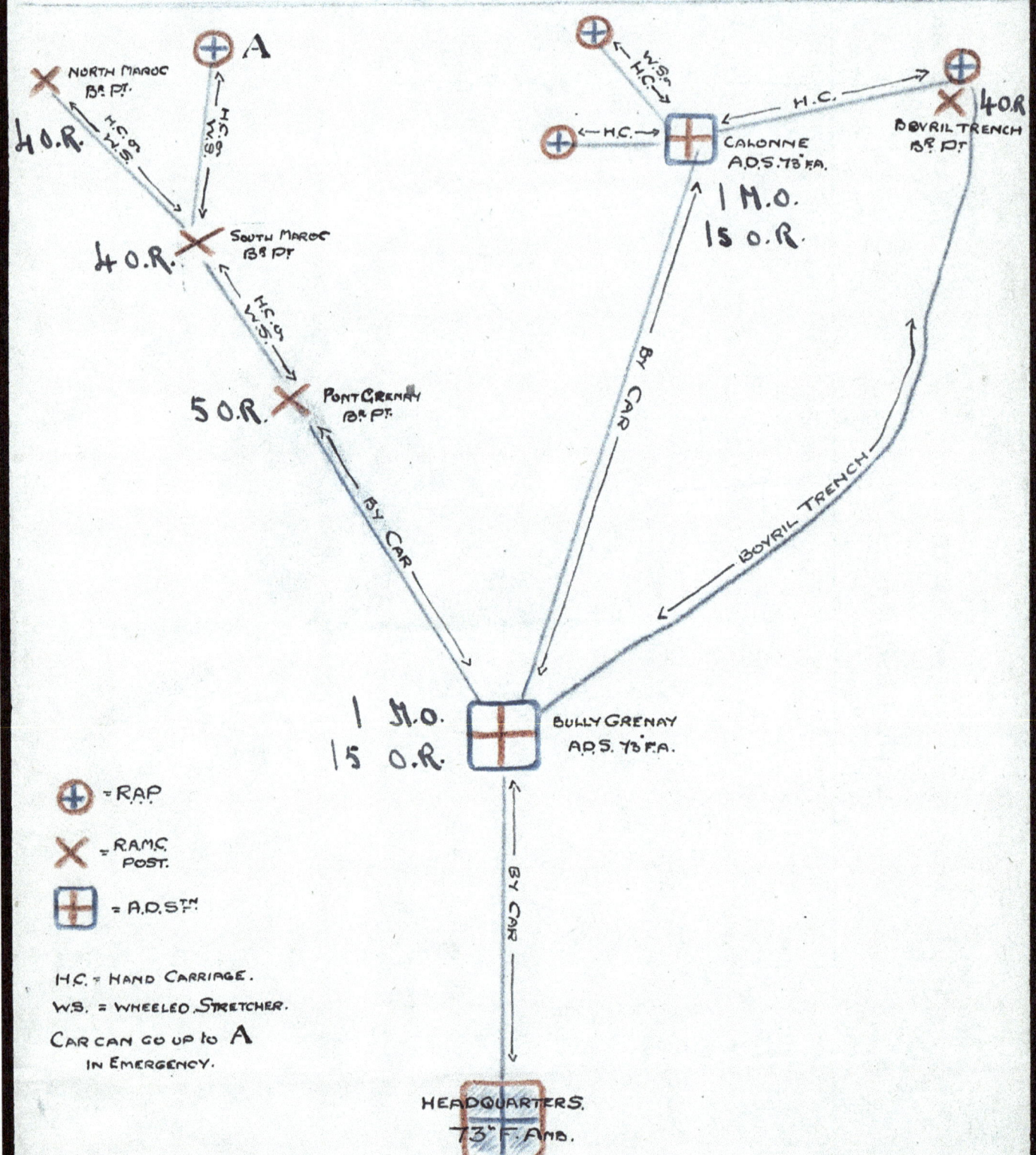

73rd Field Ambulance

COPY. 3

Movement Orders — Part 1.

B. Section will take over A.D.S.s at BULLY-GRENAY, PONT GRENAY, & collecting posts, on the afternoon of MARCH 2nd.

CAPT. BIDEN, & CAPT. WILSON (M.C.) with Sgt. Shee, Sgt Darrell, L.Cpl Martin, Ptes. Webb, Farmer, & Smith J, will proceed in 2 Sunbeams at 1.30 p.m. & report to M.O. i/c A.D.S. BULLY GRENAY, for the purposes of taking over.

At 1.30 p.m., the "m" personnel, with transport of "B" section, under CAPT. BRISCO, will march to BULLY GRENAY. After the transport is unloaded, the transport will return to headquarters.

CAPT. BRISCO will return independently.

All trench stores will be taken over, & a list forwarded to this office.

Completion of relief will be reported to this office

Personnel at A.D.S.s & outposts. ("B" Section)
BULLY GRENAY. &c

CAPT. BIDEN   CAPT. WILSON M.C.
S.Sgt. ASH, Sgt AIKEN, Sgt DARRELL, Sgt SHEE.
Cpl. Lemon, Cpl Lamont, Cpl Monk, L.Cpl Webb, L.Cpl Martin,
Ptes. Addie, Ashton, Beattie, Bricklebank, Broadbridge, Buck,
Cassidy J, Carruthers, Cockerill, Condon, Culy, Decker, Finch,
Anderson A.E, Farrell, Gibbon, Greatorex, Green, Holland P.J, Farmer,
Holland R.J, Horwood, Hunter, Judge, Jackson H, Logan, Marshall

Personnel (cont'd)

Ptes. McFarlane, Mawson, Nolan, Patterson, Peddie, ~~Rutherford~~ Butterfield, Seymour, Sharp, Sorrell, Smith J, Sparrow, Stokes, Stride, Watters, West, Whalley, ? Woollard.

Four wheeled stretchers will be taken to BULLY GRENAY.

One bicycle will be kept at PONT GRENAY

One Motor cycle to be at BULLY GRENAY when available.

J. W. Cunningham
Lieut. Col. R.A.M.C.
O.C. 73rd Fld. Amb.

1.3.17.

Copy No. (1) File
(2) Brig. Major
(3 & 4) War Diary
(5) 3rd Canadian F.A.
(6-10) All officers 73 F.A.
(11) Sgt. Major

73rd Field Ambulance.

Movement Orders.   Part 2.

73rd Field Ambce will take over the Boys School, BRAQUEMONT, from the 50th Field Amb. as the Main Dressing Station, on March 3rd.

The u/m will form the advanced party, leaving NOEUX LES MINES at 7.30 A.M.

CAPT. BRISCO (MEDICAL WARDS)   CAPT. MILNE (SURGICAL WARDS)
S.M. NEWTON,   S.Sgt COOPER,   SGT. BRASON,   SGT. JACKSON,
S.Sgt BRUCE,   S.M. MUSTART,   SGT. LUMGAIR,   CPL. BELAIN
CPL. PRECIOUS,   CPL. RICHARDSON,   L.CPL. WEBB,   L.CPL. CRAVEN.
Ptes. Airey, Ashton, Cockerill, Finlay, Gibson, Golder,
Gregson, Hamilton, Lamb, McLellan, Price, Skillington,
& Webb.

The transport will accompany the advanced party.

The remainder of the Field Ambce. under CAPT. WEIGALL, after tidying up billets & handing over to the Town Major, will follow the advanced party as soon as possible.

CAPT. WEIGALL will arrange with the Town Major, & the Mayor of NOEUX LES MINES for the necessary handing over of Government property, settling of claims, if any, & will obtain a certificate from the Mayor that all claims for damages have been duly settled.

2.3.17

W. Cunningham
Lieut. Col. R.A.M.C.
O.C. 73rd Fd. Amb.

SKETCH PLAN. LINE OF EVACUATION.
73ʳᵈ FIELD AMBULCE

from 2/3/17 to 22/3/17

DIAGRAMMATICAL.

FRONT LINE.

- CALONNE Post 73 F.A. — 12 O.R.
- 4 O.R. (Wheeled Stretcher)
- 4 O.R. (Trench Stretcher by Hand)
- 4 O.R. (Ditto)
- 4 O.R.
- 1 M.O. 10 O.R. — PONT GRENAY. A.D.S. 73 F.A.
- 1 M.O. 14 O.R. — BULLY GRENAY. A.D.S. 73 F.A.
- RAILWAY
- Evacuation by Car
- HEADQUARTERS 73ʳᵈ F. Amb.

Legend:
- ⊕ = R.A. Post.
- ⊞ (red) = Adv. Dress. Station.
- ⊞ (blue) = H.Qrs.
- ✗ = R.A.M.C. Post.

140/2086

24th Div.

73rd F.A.

COMMITTEE FOR THE
MEDICAL HISTORY OF THE WAR
Date -6 JUN.1917

Army Form C. 2118

WAR DIARY
or
INTELLIGENCE SUMMARY

43 Field Ambulance
April 1917 — Page 1

Vol 20

Place	Date	Hour	Summary of Events and Information	Remarks and references to Appendices
BRADUENONT	1-4-17		Visits A.D.S. RUDDY BREMAY. It has been chilly several times lately but none has been hurt. Arrange that an funnels shorts state in the billows. Otherwise general Routine — York	
"	2.4.17		Army Lofm formalin inspected this unit. Captain Ruddin reports his arrival for duty - after sick leave. Capt. Hewitt appointed for Company duty a Capt. Williams for permanent duty. Orderly Routine. A.D.M.S. moved to B. recapment	
"	3.4.17		Lient Price and party of 10 N.C.O's & men proceeded to No 33 C.C.S. for special duty.	
	5.4.17		A.D.M.S orders to be ready to move at short notice. Lecture on Gas & Treatment by Col. Sultan. Conference of A.D.M.S's & O.C.s Fd. Amb. afterwards.	

Army Form C. 2118

73rd Fld Ambulance

WAR DIARY
or
INTELLIGENCE SUMMARY

April 1917. Page 11

(Erase heading not required.)

Place	Date	Hour	Summary of Events and Information	Remarks and references to Appendices
BRAQUEMONT	6.4.17		1st Relief of staff at A.D.S's - B.Pn. Capt Rucklin relieved Capt Milne & Capt Baines relieved Lieut. Crimp. Pte Coleman replaced Pte Sewell at 33 C.C.S. Shelling of Bully Grenay A.D.S continues severe. Several gas shells (phosgene?) have been put over as well.	
	7.4.17		Under A.D.M.S' instruction Lieut Crimp proceeded for duty to 33 C.C.S. and much of the strength Lieut Price returned and taken on the strength. Visited BULLY GRENAY A.D.S. PONT GRENAY & CALONNE A.D.S.	
	8.4.17		2nd relief of A.D.S. - B.Pn. 1 Sgt - 16 men relieved for duty & taken on strength. Arrangements for collection & dealing with walking wounded up to 1,000 out guard for cases completed	
	9.4.17		Lieut Price & 20 men proceeded to 74th F.D. for temporary duty.	

WAR DIARY

73rd Fld Ambulance

INTELLIGENCE SUMMARY April 1917

Place	Date	Hour	Summary of Events and Information	Remarks
BRAQUEMONT	10/4/17		Lieut Price & 20 men returned from 74th F.A.	JKhl
	11/4/17		Unit visited by D.D.M.S. of 1st Corps. Lieut Price proceeded to Calonne.	
			Capt Wilson returned from leave & reported to A.D.M.S. and taken to Cauchy Stone	
	12/4/17		Lt. Col. E.W.H. Cuningham returned from leave and resumed command of the unit — Normal routine — Received 96 walking wounded cases as result of the operations on & near Right of Division — All evacuated immediately to	JKhl
			C.C.S. after being dressed fed & warmed etc.	
			Capt Wilson reports his departure to 1st Cavalry Division.	
	13/4/17		Reports that Germans are retiring in front of the Division — Keeping clear & ready to move at any short notice — Have received news in the work of a general move forward to get in touch with the 4th & 3rd Brigade & follow them notices of showing the 4th on Right & part of ≡ 14th on the centre.	JKhl

/3² Field Ambulance   April 1914   Army Form C. 2118

WAR DIARY
or
INTELLIGENCE SUMMARY

Page IV

(Erase heading not required.)

Instructions regarding War Diaries and Intelligence
Summaries are contained in F.S. Regs., Part II.
and the Staff Manual respectively. Title Pages
will be prepared in manuscript.

Place	Date	Hour	Summary of Events and Information	Remarks and references to Appendices
BRAQUEMONT	14-4-14		General advance on this front. Have fixed forward the A.D.S. to CALONNE as skeleton Bearer in conjunction with move of battalions of 12ᵗʰ + 17ᵗʰ Brigade with whom we are in touch. Reinforced 'B' section with 1 N.C.O. and 20 Bearers. Visits Calonne A.D.S. + some of R.A.M.C. Posts. See Situation Report attached. J. Kehoe	Map 36 C Afternoon Situation Report
"	15-4-14		Advance continues. Very long carry to Bearers as roads etc quite impossible for stone or Motor Ambulance in front of Calonne. Capt. RUBKIN transmitted HEVIN to find a feasible means A.D.S. Received orders to follow up the 14ᵗʰ Brigade only as subsidies of the 43ʳᵈ Brigade - One section of 42ⁿᵈ Field Ambulance took over frontage of 43ʳᵈ Brigade + all civilian patients at CALONNE who were termed in hospital. J. Kehoe	

13 Field Ambulance April 1914

WAR DIARY or INTELLIGENCE SUMMARY

Army Form C. 2118

Page 34

Place	Date	Hour	Summary of Events and Information	Remarks and references to Appendices
BRAQUANT	16-4-14		Visits CALONNE A.D.S. & B.A.H.C. Posts on the way to LIEVIN. Opens an A.D.S. at LIEVIN. and pushes further forward than Stretcher bearers — Sent up from H.Q. nine 2 N.C.O.'s and 14 men as bearers — See Situation report attached. Extra Bearers — See Situation report attached.	Stop 36 R 1-40000 Sketch Report attached
"	14-4-14		A Section from 12th Field Ambulance arrived and took over the Bully GRENAY St GRENAY and MAROC during the course of yesterday and last night. hitherto the personnel of this unit was sent them to LIEVIN when help was urgently needed there from the long distances & difficulties of ground thrown the number of casualties. Also sent up 2 N.C.Os + 16 men from H.Q.- Si: later proceeded to No. 12 General Hospital + Struck off the strength.	

№ 3 Field Ambulance

WAR DIARY or INTELLIGENCE SUMMARY

Army Form C. 2118

April 1917

Place	Date	Hour	Summary of Events and Information	Remarks and references to Appendices
BRAQUEMONT	18-4-17		Heard of impending reserve + that whole 'C' section were to proceed to rest area. 'A + B' were to be attached to No 9 C.C.S. at BRAQUEMONT. Advance parts of 9 C.C.S. came to take over. Relieved Capt. Ruskin + some of 'C' section from here — sent to rest. Major Milne up. Wounds admitted during day — some. O.R.s O.R. 480.	
	19-4-17		Lieut. Swire + remainder of 'C' into rear in line returned to rest. Several wounded admitted — some attended.	
	20-4-17		Relief completed — all advance parties handed over to 40th Division + Main dressing station to 9 C.C.S. — A + B remain attached to rest area to 9 C.C.S. as 'C' section wounded to rest area with 13. Bridge under Capt. Wigan — Capt. Milne proceeds to No 9 Reserve Park A.S.C. + struck off the strength.	
	21-4-17		All the men given a rest today — victo A.D.M.S. at NEPPENT Farms.	

Army Form C. 2118.

73rd Field Ambulance

April 1917

WAR DIARY
or
INTELLIGENCE SUMMARY

(Erase heading not required.)

Page viii

Instructions regarding War Diaries and Intelligence Summaries are contained in F.S. Regs., Part II. and the Staff Manual respectively. Title Pages will be prepared in manuscript.

Place	Date	Hour	Summary of Events and Information	Remarks and references to Appendices
BRAQUEMONT	22-4-17		Church Parade – Nothing of importance to note.	
	23-4-17		N.C.O's + men detailed to various duties at 7 C.C.S.	
	24-4-17		General routine – Nil of importance.	
	25-4-17		"	
	26-4-17		" Received orders to send 5 water carts temporary duty to D.D.M.S. hdqrs.	
	27-4-17		" "C" Section returned to Houchin.	
	28-4-17		" Nil of importance.	
	29-4-17		A.D.M.S. visits the F.A. left at Braquemont + sections at Houchin.	
	30-4-17		General Routine – Details to man the permanent duty with Heavy Artillery Groups + struck them off the strength. Visits 9.0.C. 73rd Brigade and "C" section at Houchin.	

John Cunningham
Lt. Col.
O.C. 73rd F.A.

COPY.

B.E.F.

SUMMARY OF MEDICAL WAR DIARIES of

73rd Field Ambulance,

24th Division,

    1st Corps, 1st Army, till 21.4.17.
    2nd Corps, 1st Army, from 21.4.17.-10.5.17.
    2nd Corps, 2nd Army, from 10.5.17.

WESTERN FRONT, APRIL - MAY, 1917.

O.C. Lt.Colonel F. W. M. Cuningham.

SUMMARISED UNDER THE FOLLOWING HEADINGS:-

Phase "B" - Battle of Arras. "April - May, 1917."

1st Period, April 1917. Attack on Vimy Ridge.
2nd Period, May, 1917. Capture of Siegfried Line.

73rd F.A., 24th Division, B.E.F. Western Front,
O.C. Lt.Col. F. W. M. Cuningham. April 1917.
1st Corps, 1st Army.

Phase "B" - Battle of Arras. "April - May, 1917."
1st Period, April 1917. Attack on Vimy Ridge.

April	H.Q. at Braquemont. (36c)
6th	**Operations Enemy, & Ops. Enemy Gas.** Shelling of Bully Grenay continued severe. Several gas shells included.
7th	**Med. Arr.** Location of A.D.S;- 1. Bully Grenay 2. Pont Grenay 3. Calonne Attached App. 1. (copy)
8th	Arrangements completed for collecting and dealing with Wlkg. W. up to 1000 and gassed W.
9th	**Moves det.** 1 & 20 to 74th F.A. returned 10th inst.
12th	**Operations & Casualties** Operations on extreme R. of Divn. 96 Wlkg. W.
14th	**Operations** General advance. **Med. Arr.** A.D.S. moved forward to Calonne and Str. Brs. in conjunction with move of Batlns. of 72 & 17th Bdes. with whom Unit was in touch. B. section reinforced by 1 & 20 Brs. Attached App. 1 A. (Put back in Diary.)
15th	**Operations** Advance continued. **Evacuation** Very long carry for Brs. **Terrain** Roads impassable to H. and M. Ambs. in front of Calonne. **Med. Arr.** 1 section 72nd F.A. took over front of 72nd Bde. and personnel of 73rd F.A. rejoined at Calonne (Attached App. 2)
16th	A.D.S. opened at Liévin. Str. Brs. pushed further forward. Attached App. 1 B. (copy) (Put back in Diary)
17th	**Med. Arr.** Section 72nd F.A. took over Bully Grenay, Pt. Grenay, and Maroc. Personnel relieved, sent to Liévin. **Evacuation & Casualties** Very long carry and difficult ground. Not large numbers.
19th-20th	**Military Situation & Med. Arr.** Attached App. 3. (Put back in Diary)
20th	**Med. Arr.** Relief completed. All adv. P's handed over to 46th/

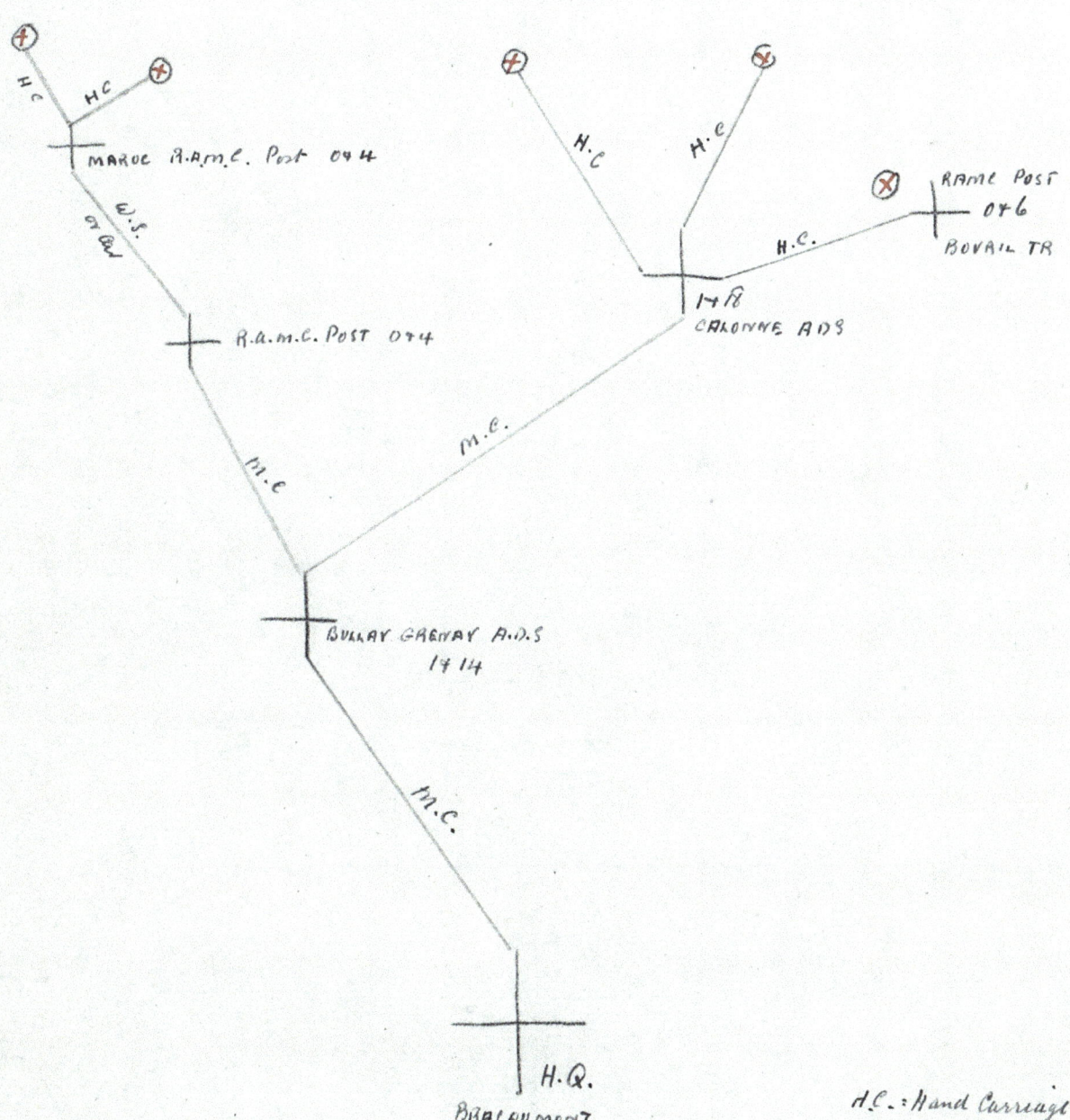

73 F.A. Lines of Evacuation
7.4.19

1.

2.

Front Line

Supports

⊕ O.8   ⊕ O.8   ⊕ O.8
  Post   Post   Post
      H.C.   H.C.   H.C.

      LIEVIN   2+20
       ADS
              + O+12
                 Post
       Partly H.C. W.S.
       total low lying
              + O+8
                 Post

              + O+8
                 Post

      CALONNE + 2+14
        ADS

           M.C.

           +
          H.Q.
                          H.C. Hand Carriage
                          W.S. Wh. Sti
⊕ RAP.   BRACQUEMONT   M.C. Motor Am-

73 F.A.   Route of Evacuation

                        14.4.19

73rd F.A., 24th Division, B.E.F.   Western Front.

O.C. Lt.Col. F. W. M. Cuningham.   April 1917.

1st Corps, 1st Army, till 21.4.17.   2.
2nd Corps, from 21.4.17.

Phase "B", continued.

1st Period, continued.

April 20th (contd.)	H.Q. at Braquemont.
	Med. Arr. contd. 46th Divn. M.D.S. handed over to 7th C.C.S.
	A. and B. sections attached to 7th C.C.S.
	C. section to Rest Area.
21st	Transfer To 2nd Corps Area.
21st-30th	Nothing of note.

73rd F.A., 24th Division, B.E.F. (All Apps. attached to 1st copies.)
O.C. Lt.Col. F. W. M. Cuningham.
1st Corps, 1st Army.

Western Front,
April 1917.
1.

Phase "B" - Battle of Arras. "April - May, 1917."
1st Period, April 1917. Attack on Vimy Ridge.

April	H.Q. at Braquemont. (36c)
6th	<u>Operations Enemy, & Ops. Enemy Gas.</u> Shelling of Bully Grenay continued severe. Several gas shells included.
7th	<u>Med. Arr.</u> Location of A.D.S;-
	1. Bully Grenay
	2. Pont Grenay
	3. Calonne Attached App. 1.
8th	Arrangements completed for collecting and dealing with Wlkg. W. up to 1000 and gassed W.
9th	<u>Moves det.</u> 1 & 20 to 74th F.A. returned 10th inst.
12th	<u>Operations & Casualties</u> Operations on extreme R. of Divn. 96 Wlkg. W.
14th	<u>Operations</u> General advance.
	<u>Med. Arr.</u> A.D.S. moved forward to Calonne and Str. Brs. in conjunction with move of Batlns. of 72 & 17th Bdes. with whom Unit was in touch. B. section reinforced by 1 & 20 Brs. Attached App. 1 A.
15th	<u>Operations</u> Advance continued.
	<u>Evacuation</u> Very long carry for Brs.
	<u>Terrain</u> Roads impassable to H. and M. Ambs. in front of Calonne
	<u>Med. Arr.</u> 1 section 72nd F.A. took over front of 72nd Bde. and personnel of 73rd F.A. rejoined at Calonne (Attached App. 2
16th	A.D.S. opened at Liévin. Str. Brs. pushed further forward. Attached App. 1 B.
17th	<u>Med. Arr.</u> Section 72nd F.A. took over Bully Grenay, Pt. Grenay, and Maroc. Personnel relieved, sent to Liévin.
	<u>Evacuation & Casualties</u> Very long carry and difficult ground. Not large numbers.
19th-20th	<u>Military Situation & Med. Arr.</u> Attached App. 3.
20th	<u>Med. Arr.</u> Relief completed. All adv. P's handed over to 46th/

73rd F.A., 24th Division, B.E.F.   Western Front.

O.C. Lt.Col. F. W. M. Cuningham.   April 1917.

1st Corps, 1st Army, till 21.4.17.   2.
2nd Corps, from 21.4.17.

Phase "B", continued.

1st Period, continued.

April 20th (contd.)	H.Q. at Braquemont.
	Med. Arr. contd. 46th Divn. M.D.S. handed over to 7th C.C.S.
	A. and B. sections attached to 7th C.C.S.
	C. section to Rest Area.
21st	Transfer To 2nd Corps Area.
21st-30th	Nothing of note.

73rd Field Ambulance.
Diagrammatical Sketch of Evacuation.

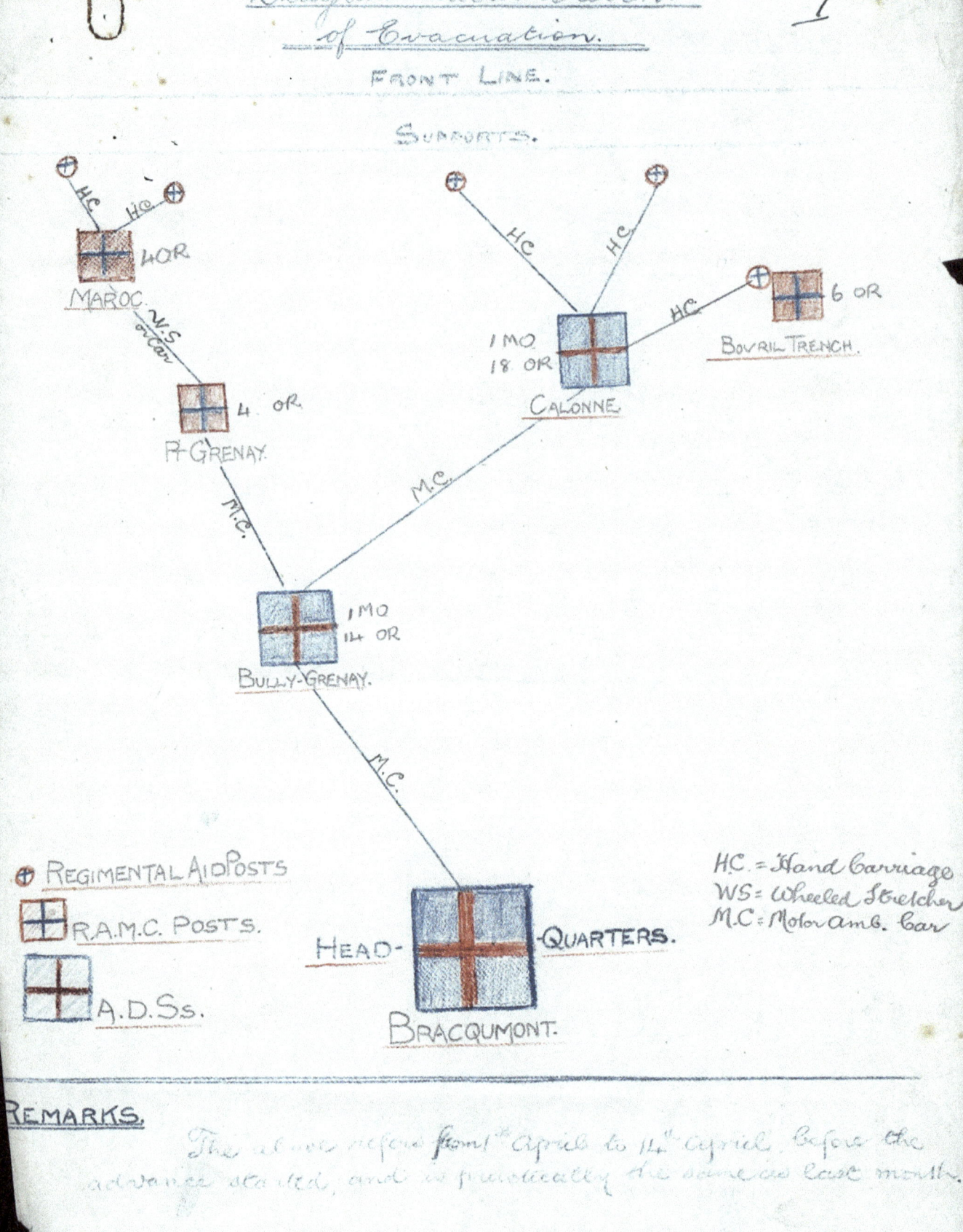

Legend:
- ⊕ Regimental Aid Posts
- R.A.M.C. Posts
- A.D.Ss.

- H.C. = Hand Carriage
- W.S. = Wheeled Stretcher
- M.C. = Motor Amb. Car

REMARKS.

The above refers from 1st April to 14th April, before the advance started, and is practically the same as last month.

SECRET.

1A.

The situation of "B" Section 73rd Field Ambulance and communication with our R. M.Os at 6pm this evening are as follows :-

ADVANCED DRESSING STATION. Calonne. 14-c-8-9.
    2 Sunbeam Cars.   2 M.O.s and staff.

RAMC POST.   Maroc.   M.3-d-2-1.
    1 Sunbeam and 1 Ford Car. 1 Sergeant and 10 men.
    Cases evacuated direct to Bracquemont.

RAMC POST.   In touch with West Kents. M.16-b-5-6.

RAMC POST.   In touch with 3rd R.B.   M.21-d-10-5.

RAMC POST.   In touch with North Staffs. Old Aid Post in Essex Lane
    In communication with E. Surreys, who are due east of then
    Position not exactly located, but believed to be good dug-outs.

RAMC POST.   In touch with West Surreys Aid Post.
    Approximately M.17-a-3-9.

Evacuation along the Railway and thence across the open to Calonne, the relief post being rear to where the Railway cuts the old German front line approximately M.15-b-6-3.

One private holds the old A.D.S. at Bully Grenay and Pont Grenay respectively.

The four bearers at Maroc North have been withdrawn and sent to assist at M.21-d-10-5.

Captain Williams and two nursing orderlies are being sent to Bully Grenay to hold the place, at 9pm tonight.

14/4/17.

Lt.Col.RAMC.
Commanding 73rd Field Amb.

Situation report 73rd Field Ambulance in front line area at
6 pm this evening is as follows :-

M.Os.i/c A.D.Ss. are in touch with all R.M.Os of 17th
Brigade and the Brigade Major of the 17th I.B., also they are
receiving some cases from some R.M.Os. on the left and right
of Calonne.

A.D.S. CALONNE. 14-c-8-9. 2 M.Os. and nursing staff.

A.D.S. LIEVIN. Approximately C.22-b-7-5.(Map 36c,1-40,000).

1 M.O., 1 Staff-Sergeant. and 2 nursing orderlies are
already there. A second M.O. and 2 nursing orderlies are
proceeding there tomorrow morning.

Equipment is being gradually got up there from Calonne
under difficulties.

Bearers are stationed at all of the R.A.Ps. of the Brigade,
also RAMC Posts at C-21.c-9-9. and C-22.b-9-9.

Evacuation from Lievin to Calonne partly be wheeled stretchers
partly along the Railway, using German trolleys, partly
hand carriage.

It is hoped that the road will soon be open for both
horse traffic and later for motor traffic.

More bearers are in readiness to proceed up if required
by M.Os i/c A.D.Ss.

Lt.Col.RAMC.
Commanding 73rd Field Ambulance.

16/4/17.

73rd Field Ambulance.

Diagrammatical Sketch of Evacuation.

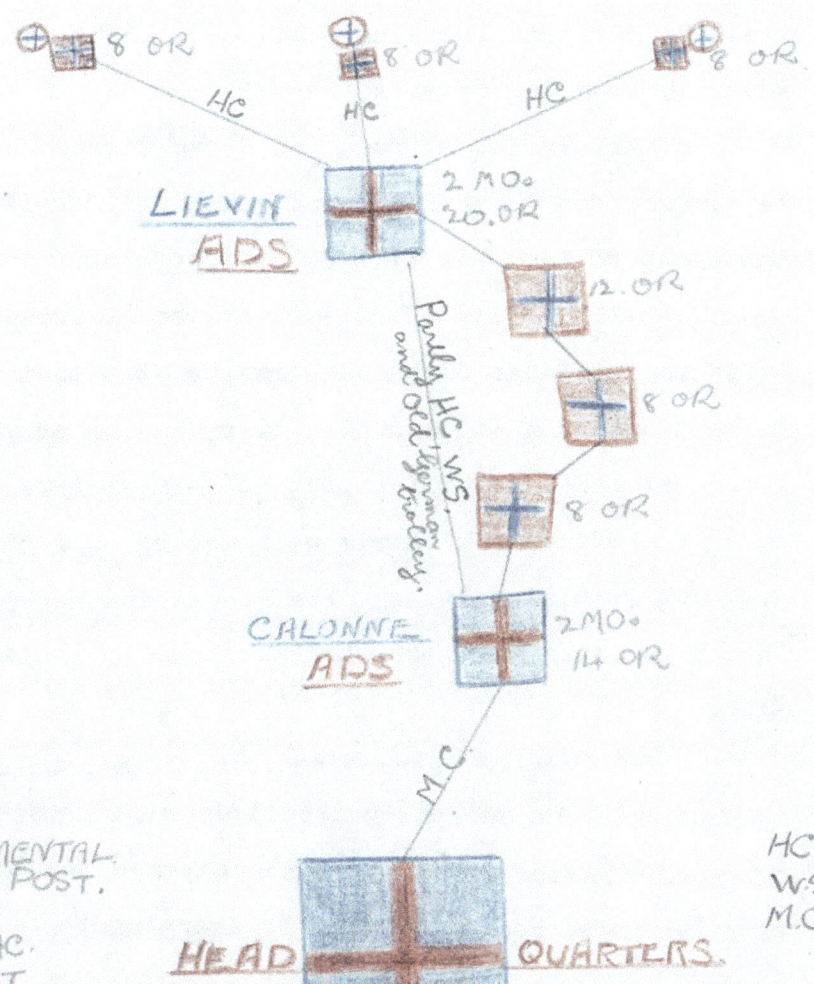

REMARKS

The above refers from April 11th to 19-20, when the unit was relieved in the front area.

73rd Field Ambulance.

MOVEMENT ORDERS.

The 24th Division will be relieved by the 46th Division, relief to be completed by midnight 19-20 April, 1917.

FRONT AREA. No. 1 North Midland Field Ambulance will take over the Advanced Dressing Station, CALONNE, and the Advanced Dressing Station, LIEVIN.

All Trench Stores, Red Cross Stores, etc, will be handed over to the incoming unit, only Mobilisation Equipment of the unit will be brought back.

All details of relief will be arranged between the Officers in charge Advanced Dressing Stations, receipts to be taken of what is handed over, and on completion personnel and cars will report to Headquarters, Bracquemont.

Officer in charge will arrange how the men are to get back to Headquarters. Preference in the returning cars should be given to those who have been up longest.

BACK AREA.

"C" Section, plus pioneer squad and several extra men who will be specially detailed, will proceed to Livossart in the rest area under Captain Weigall on the 20th instant, route and time of starting to be notified later.

[signature]
Lt. Col. RAMC.
Commanding 73rd Field Amb.

19/4/17.

140/2161

COMMITTEE FOR THE
MEDICAL HISTORY OF THE WAR
Date 10 JUL. 1917

No. 73. 7. a.

Carbons.

B.E.F.

SUMMARY OF MEDICAL WAR DIARIES of

73rd Field Ambulance,

24th Division,

    1st Corps, 1st Army, till 21.4.17.
    2nd Corps, 1st Army, from 21.4.17.-10.5.17.
    2nd Corps, 2nd Army, from 10.5.17.

WESTERN FRONT, APRIL - MAY, 1917.

O.C. Lt.Colonel F. W. M. Cuningham.

SUMMARISED UNDER THE FOLLOWING HEADINGS:-

Phase "B" - Battle of Arras. "April - May, 1917."

1st Period, April 1917. Attack on Vimy Ridge.
2nd Period, May, 1917. Capture of Siegfried Line.

<u>73rd F.A., 24th Division B.E.F.</u>　　　　　<u>Western Front.</u>

<u>O.C. Lt.Col. F. W. M. Cuningham.</u>　　　<u>May 1917.</u>

<u>2nd Corps, 1st Army, till 10.5.17.</u>　　　1.
<u>2nd Corps, 2nd Army, from 10.5.17.</u>

<u>Phase "B" - Battle of Arras. "April - May, 1917."</u>

<u>2nd Period, May, 1917. Capture of Siegfried Line.</u>

May		H.Q. at Houchin.
2nd	<u>Moves</u>	To Houchin.
8th		To Verquin.
9th		To Mt. Bernahon.
10th	<u>Moves & Transfer</u>	To Tannay, en route for 2nd Army.

73rd F.A., 24th Division B.E.F. Western Front.

O.C. Lt.Col. F. W. M. Cuningham. May 1917.

2nd Corps, 1st Army, till 10.5.17. 1.
2nd Corps, 2nd Army, from 10.5.17.

Phase "B" - Battle of Arras. "April - May, 1917."

2nd Period, May, 1917. Capture of Siegfried Line.

May		H.Q. at Houchin.
2nd	Moves	To Houchin.
8th		To Verquin.
9th		To Mt. Bernahon.
10th	Moves & Transfer	To Tannay, en route for 2nd Army.

Army Form C. 2118.

73rd Field Ambulance

WAR DIARY or **INTELLIGENCE SUMMARY**
(Erase heading not required.)

May 1917   Page 1

Place	Date	Hour	Summary of Events and Information	Remarks and references to Appendices
BRAQUEMONT	1-5-17		General Routine – Nil of importance to note.	
HOUCHIN	2-5-17		Moved Hdq. F.A. to "C" Section at Houchin. Capts Wrigall + Price detailed for duty at L.E.S. and Capt. Brisco transferred to Hdq. Qr. Du Vuge reports his arrival for duty.	
"	3-5-17		General Routine – All Box respirators tested in gas chamber by gas officer.	
"	4-5-17		General Routine.	
"	5-5-17		Arrangs. for transport on March to 4th Northampton + 13th Middlesex. Horse tramways then 2 Battalions are to be arranged by Medically by 7th F.A. and this unit in turn arranges for 3rd R.B. and 8th British. Capt. Lillimann + Surg. of Lt. G.R. returned from 7 L.E.s. Lt. Winslow reports for duty from the base Gr.	
"	6-5-17		Germans evacuates sick and struck off the strength. Capt. Williams proceeded on 14 days M.O. of Royal Sussex. Lt. GREEN departs for England to take up a commission and struck off the strength. Church Service.	
"	7-5-17		General routine – Nothing of importance to note.	
VERQUIN	8-5-17		Suddenly received orders to move to VERQUIN + recall all Ranks at L.E.s. Started at 2 p.m. and bodies from L.E.s. arrived in the evening. Reported however on arrival to join sections	

Army Form C. 2118.

73rd Field Ambulance.

WAR DIARY or INTELLIGENCE SUMMARY

May 1917

Page 11

(Erase heading not required.)

Place	Date	Hour	Summary of Events and Information	Remarks and references to Appendices
MT. BERNANCHON	9-5-17		The F.A. marched to Mt. BERNANCHON today with the Brigade. Very hot and has to pick up a lot of "fall outs" from Brigade.	
TANNAY	10-5-17		Marched to TANNAY with BRIGADE again very hot and many men fell out.	
"	11-5-17		Pte. Macfarlane + Corkhill wounds sick. Rests for the day. Pollocks local sick. Bathing Section.	
STEENVOORDE	12-5-17		Marched to Steenvoorde - Very hot long march - Pollocks sick of Brigade.	
"	13-5-17		Rests after the day. Most tedious on regards Brigade sick. H.Q. + "C" section	
DEVONSHIRE CAMP (RENINGHELST)	14-5-17		Ambulance again to be split up - two separate sub-attacks - many wounded - hand tents at 6.30 and arrived at 10. A cut wound + abrasions.	
"	15-5-17		Routine for Sick + wounded of Sick. General Routine - Hospital opened for Brigade sick.	
"	16-5-17		General Routine. F.G.C.M. on Sgt. AIKEN at H.Q. of Sussex.	
"	17-5-17		General Routine. Pte. DYER attached to D.B.M.S. X Corps for clerical duty.	
"	18-5-17		General Routine. Pte. Macfarlane returned to duty + taking on strength.	
"	19-5-17		General Routine - Nothing of importance to note -	

Army Form C. 2118.

73rd Field Ambulance WAR DIARY or INTELLIGENCE SUMMARY

May 1917 Page iii

(Erase heading not required.)

Instructions regarding War Diaries and Intelligence Summaries are contained in F.S. Regs., Part II and the Staff Manual respectively. Title Pages will be prepared in manuscript.

Place	Date	Hour	Summary of Events and Information	Remarks and references to Appendices
Bramshill Camp	20-5-17		General routine. Nothing of importance to note.	
"	21-5-17		General Routine. Detachment moved to K.28.b.6. L.A.N. Bagshaw A.S.C. reports for duty.	
"	22-5-17		General Routine.	
"	23-5-17		Capt. Williams returned from Sussex Regt. to H.Q. Pte. Boyt wounded sick. Sergeant Wilson reduced to the ranks by a F.G.C.M.	
"	24-5-17		General routine. Pte. Jones Thorn + Hutson wounded sick.	
"	25-5-17		General routine. Pte. Beatrix wounded sick.	
"	26-5-17		Detachment moved up to LEMPIRE Ferme - See special orders. Pte Macaulay + Pte Kelly awarded the M.M. F.A. Davies + Beck up today to move.	
"	27-5-17		Conference at office of A.D.M.S. as regards future active operations.	
"	28-5-17		H.Q. + "B" section moved down to L/3.2.5.g. + F.A. together again. Pte Robertson and Lanigan wounded sick. Capt. Briscoe + 6 O.R. reported to O.C. 138 F.A. for 48 hrs. duty to learn the front area.	
HEUDIKEN	29-5-17		Visits HQ bivouac area with O.C. 138 F.A. Corp. Willer wounded sick.	
"	30-5-17		Capt. Williams + 2 O.R. visits his bi- first area.	

//

WAR DIARY or INTELLIGENCE SUMMARY

Army Form C. 2118.

73 Field Ambulance
May 1919

Place	Date	Hour	Summary of Events and Information	Remarks and references to Appendices
HESDIN M3a5,1	31-5-19		Usual Routine - Nothing of importance to note. J.W. Cunningham Lt Col OC 73 FA	

OPERATION ORDERS.

73rd. Field Ambulance. 14/5/17.

"B" Section plus Headquarters will move to DEVONSHIRE CAMP on the 14th. inst.

"A" and "C" Sections under Capt. Rudkin will remain at STEENVOORDE until further orders.

TRANSPORT.

"B" Section complete plus one Water cart and one G.S. wagon from "A" Section will be at the CROSS ROADS (K.26.d. 05. 50) at 5-45 pm, and proceed independently to DEVONSHIRE CAMP under Capt. Rudkin, who will return to STEENVOORDE on completion.

"B" Section plus Headquarters will parade near Transport Lines at 6-20 pm.

Transport arrangements for the march will be notified later.

"B" Section and Headquarters will have their valises ready for packing at One o-clock.

[signature]

Lieut.Col.R.A.M.C.
Commanding 73rd. Field Ambce.

14/5/17.

Officer i/c,
    Detachment,
        73rd. Field Ambulance.
----

(1)   You are to proceed tomorrow, 26th. inst., to KENORA CAMP (M3.c.o.o.), via the Main Road (ABEELE-RENINGHELST).

(2)   Capt. Weigall is meeting the Staff Captain in the morning to fix up your billets.

(3)   A G.S. wagon will leave here at 6a.m. tomorrow morning to report to you.

(4)   Your rations will be arranged for from here to meet you at your new destination.

(5)   Detain the Sunbeam that brings these orders, and arrange that ambulance cars accompany the two battalions of the 17th. Infy.Bde. moving from STEENVOORDE on the same date as you are.

(6)   During the course of the day, send us the cyclist to notify me of the approximate time you expect to arrive.

                                    Lt.Col.R.A.M.C.
                            Commanding 73rd. Fld.Ambce.

25/517.

140/2230

No. 73. T.a.

June 1917.

COMMITTEE FOR THE
MEDICAL HISTORY OF THE WAR
Date — 7 AUG. 1917

Army Form C. 2118.

43rd Field Ambulance

WAR DIARY
or
INTELLIGENCE SUMMARY

(Erase heading not required.)

Map 28
June 1917
Page 1

Place	Date	Hour	Summary of Events and Information	Remarks and references to Appendices
BENINQHURST	1-6-17		The unit moved here today & is under canvas alongside 138 F.A. Arrsts. Visited Camp & discussed future operations.	
"	2-6-17		General Rostwick. Corp. Bellin proceeded to 3. R.B. for permanent water duty. 4 O.R. ranks proceeded to front area for 48 hr. instruction. Visited 73. J.B. to talk over medical arrangements in coming offensive.	
"	3-6-17		General Rostwick.	
"	4-6-17		Me Capt. Buisco & brigade proceed to the Brigade Ammly line to examine position & arrange transport. Swan Chateau — Segard Chateau. Pte HEALE proceeded to 9.31.b.1.9 for divisional water duty. Pte Gibbs transd & remants to L.b.S.	
"	5-6-17		Took over building etc. from 138 F.A. Visits Brigade to make final medical arrangements. Conference at St. O's before field order.	
"	6-6-17		12 tons of the Boar attacks to the Stretcher Bearers. The Brown Division under Capt. Buisco - left for assembly point.	

Army Form C. 2118.

WAR DIARY
or
INTELLIGENCE SUMMARY (Erase heading not required.)

73rd Field Ambulance   Map 28   June 1917   Page 11

Place	Date	Hour	Summary of Events and Information	Remarks and references to Appendices
RENINGHELST	June 7–9		Time here for the 41st Division was 3.10 a.m. and for 24th Division 3.10 p.m. — The offensive to prepare. Visited the sections in M.D. forward stand at 1 p.m. — gave them they extra UTCDS with the attacking Battalion to the shooting off front. — On return ordered up extra stretchers and still dressing + lotion etc as we saw supply of N.Y.D. been evidently not going to be sufficient for the one brought by the two divisions. On arriving of 1st advance to Y.C.1 R.A.P. & O.R. to learn on advanced dressing station with a large supply of dressings, ether, bonito + splints + Morphia which was all that could be done here. — Though casualties of our own Brigade were very small during the actual attack + consideration of the Reserve Klept bay for 24 hours on no helping the wounded of the division in but stuff. — German prisoners found very useful in helping the wounded down the trolley line —	See operation orders, diagrammatic plan of evacuation + summary of actual attack.—

/3" Field Ambulance.

WAR DIARY or INTELLIGENCE SUMMARY Map 28 + Map 27. June 1914 Page iii

Army Form C. 2118.

Place	Date	Hour	Summary of Events and Information	Remarks and references to Appendices
REMINGHELST	10-6-14		Up to now the only ride the men have had, has been arranged for by M.O. He Beam + consists of a few hours climb in our old grate lanes. The remedies for this have not have long but the troat say boys owing to the key short sick from not the character of the ground. Am now withdrawing them each day + partly replacing them from the best division which is sent except for times sick from have units—	
"	11-6-14		Shoots the relief of front line in conjunction with 41st Division Relief completed + all 43rd F.A. clubs at Remenghelst	
"	12-6-14		The unit intends here today to open a D.R.S.	
Map 24 R2.0.8.9	13-6-14		Observe Routine in planning the camp for a divisional training school —	
"	14-6-14		Many attractions necessary —	
"	15-6-14		Capt. Price proceeds to Stottesden for temporary duty The work on the Camp programme	

Army Form C. 2118.

42nd Field Ambulance

WAR DIARY
or
INTELLIGENCE SUMMARY

Stop 24
June 1917
Page IV

(Erase heading not required.)

Instructions regarding War Diaries and Intelligence Summaries are contained in F. S. Regs., Part II. and the Staff Manual respectively. Title Pages will be prepared in manuscript.

Place	Date	Hour	Summary of Events and Information	Remarks and references to Appendices
R.2.a.8.9	16-6-17		General Routine. Capt. Allen & Lt. Mitchell taken on the strength.	
	17-6-17		" D.D.M.S. X Corps & D.A.D. Division visited Camp.	
	18-6-17		C.R.E. X Corps visited Camp & arranged for necessary material to improve & enlarge the Camp as a D.R.S.	
	19-6-17		General Routine.	
	20-6-17		G.O.C. Division visited Camp.	
	21-6-17		General Routine.	
	22-6-17		Capt. Allen & 30 O.R. proceeds to 42 F.A. for temporary duty up the line.	
	23/6/17 24 25 26		General Routine. Steady progress with Camp improvements.	
	27/6/17		Capt. Allen & 30 O.R. returned from 42 after a very strenuous time up the line - G. Hills was evacuated wounded.	
	28/6/17 29 30		General Routine.	

J H Jennings Lam
Lt. Col. R.A.M.C.
O.C. 42nd F.A.

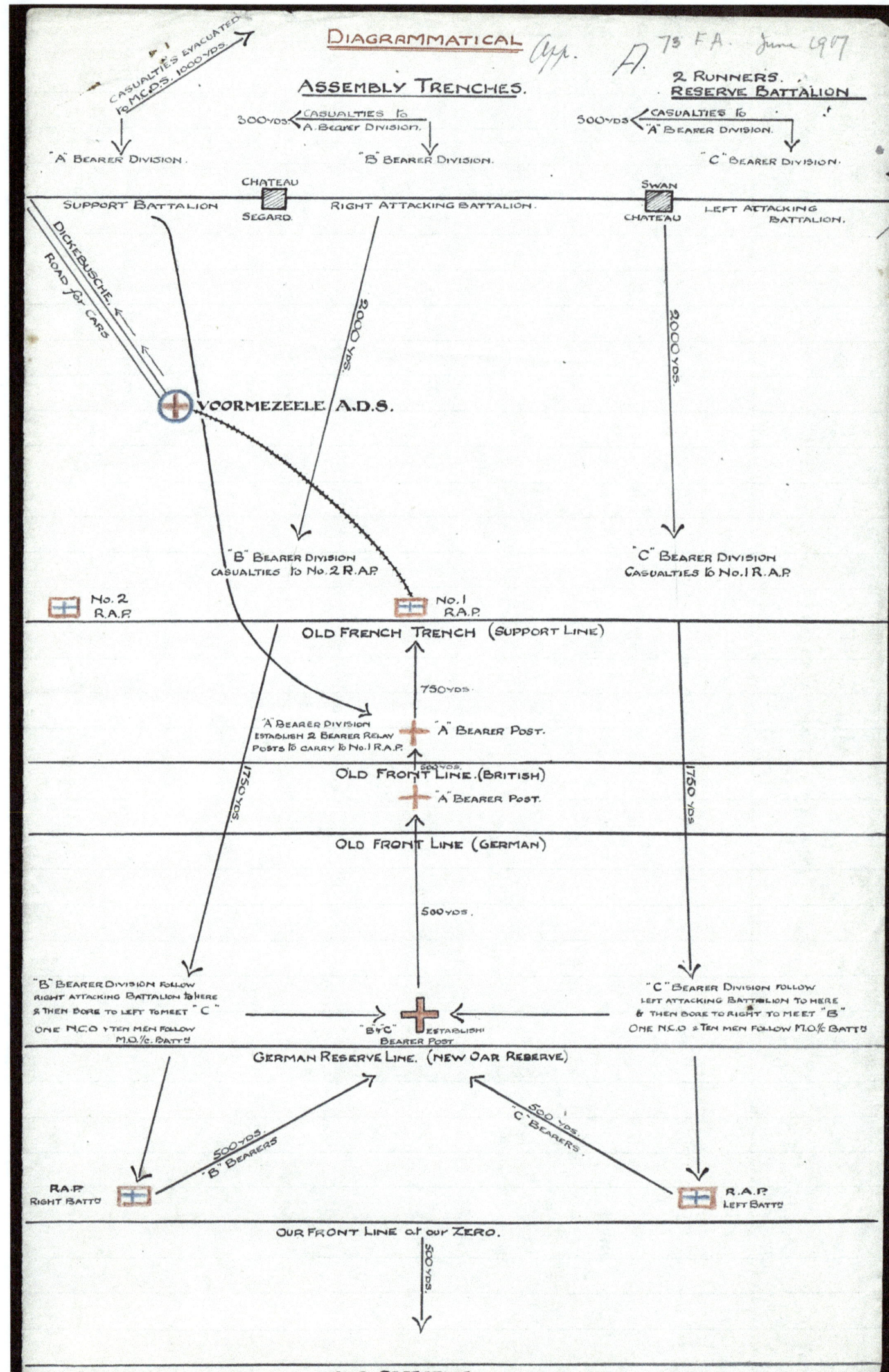

6-6-17   June 1917.   App A.1.

OPERATION ORDER — 73rd FIELD AMBULANCE.

1. The Bearer Division of 73rd Field Ambulance will be attached to the 73rd Brigade, and will move with them from the point of assembly.
   The services of the bearers will be reserved as far as possible until the 73rd Brigade is engaged from "Black" line onwards.

2. The Tent Division will remain closed, but packed and ready to move.

3. Captain Brisco will be in charge of all the bearers on the Brigade frontage and co-ordinate the work of the three sub-divisions.

4. "C" Subdivision will report at the Middlesex Camp, H.13.c.3.9. on the 6th instant by 7 p.m.
   "B" Subdivision will report to the Sussex Camp, H.13.c.3.4. by 7 p.m.
   "A" Subdivision, plus the Band stretcher bearers will report at the Leinster Camp, G.24.c.6.5. at 7 p.m.
   Captain Brisco will accompany "C" and Captain Weigall "A".

5. Subdivisions will accompany the Battalions to the points of assembly. As Battalions leave the assembly point, the M.O. in charge of bearers will detail two reliable runners for each R.M.O. In addition he will detail one N.C.O. and eight men to accompany the R.M.O. of each Battalion taking part in the attack, and these men will work from the R.A.P. back to the first R.A.M.C. Post which he forms (probably about the line of Damm Strasse).
   Further posts, the number depending on circumstances, will be formed by him up to the most advanced collecting post of the 41st Division (138 Field Ambulance) who are then responsible for evacuation of the wounded.

6. Bearers must never go beyond the respective points between which they are working, and the relay system must be adhered to. As a general rule, two men must suffice for each stretcher case between the various posts, but over exceptionally difficult ground the M.O. or N.C.O. will arrange for three or more as he considers necessary. Walking cases should be directed from post to post until they reach the zone worked by 41st Division.

7. Casualties occurring between the assembly point and Old French Trench will be notified by runner to "A" Sub-division following the Leinsters, and taken to the nearest medical post of the 48th Division as per map attached.
Casualties occurring between Old French Trench and "Black" line will be evacuated by "B" & "C" Sub-Divisions. The RAMC bearers accompanying the RMO of the Battalions should be reserved for work from the R.A.P.

8. Before leaving Headquarters, each bearer sub-division will be issued with 12 extra stretchers and slings, and all available shell dressing haversacks and water bottles will be divided between the three sub-divisions. Each bearer will keep his own pair of slings and is responsible for them. Stretchers will be exchanged at the various posts.

9. Captain Rudkin will be attached to Brigade Headquarters, & to keep in touch with Captain Prideo in front, and be ready to take over charge of the reserve stretcher bearers which the Brigade have promised in the event of heavy casualties.

10. O.C. 73rd Field Ambulance, with one motor cyclist and one orderly, will probably have his Headquarters at the advanced Headquarters of O.C. 139 Field Ambulance, which will be at Dickebusch at Zero hour, but this will be definitely announced later.

11. 50% of the Band will be attached to Captain Weigall (A Sub-division). Their probable work will be the evacuation of stretcher cases to the nearest Medical Post (see para. 7) between the assembly point and Old French Trench.

12. Two days rations will be carried, and further arrangements will be made as the situation develops.

13. A supply of water in Petrol Tins is being arranged for by 41st Division at Nos 1 and 2 R.A.P. as per attached map.
There are water points at the following places:-
I 31. d. 3.9.
I 31. d. 2.9.

14. Extra stretchers or other supplies can also be obtained from 41st Division posts, and these will be replaced by arrangements between O.Cs. 138 and 73rd Field Ambulances.

15. Medical arrangements 784/57! dated 4.6.17. Information regarding the position of various medical posts of 41st, 47th and 23rd Divisions, will be published separately to all M.Os concerned.

John Pennington
Lieut-Colonel RAMC
O.C. 73rd Field Amb^{ce}

Copies to:-
1. File
2.3. War Diary
4. 73rd Inf. Bde.
5. ADMS
6. OC. 138 Field Amb^{ce}
7-15 M.Os

73rd F.A.
June 1917

App B

A.D.M.S. 24th Divn.

REPORT ON OPERATIONS - 73 FLD AMBULANCE.

A. B. and C. Bearer Sub-Sections reached the assembling point of the 73rd Inf. Bde under Capt. Brisco between 1 and 2 a.m. Two runners, 1 N.C.O., and 8 men detailed to Middlesex, Sussex, and Leinster Regts. Two runners to Northants Regt.

B. and C. Sub-Sections under Capt. Brisco proceeded from the assembling point behind the Middlesex and Sussex at 11-30 a.m., and reached OLD FRENCH TRENCH about 1 p.m. Few casualties, all of which were easily dealt with.

A. Sub-Section moved up to OLD FRENCH TRENCH behind the Leinsters about 3-0 p.m.

At 1-45 p.m. B. and C. Sections followed the Middlesex and Sussex from OLD FRENCH TRENCH as far as the DAMM STRASSE, where the two Sections met and formed Bearer Posts.

Captain WEIGALL with reserves formed posts between the OLD FRENCH TRENCH and the above-mentioned posts. The casualties of the Brigade were few and easily dealt with, but the other Sub-Sections and 12 of the Band who were attached, were working all night assisting wounded other than those of our own Brigade.

On the morning of the 8th, the Leinsters and Northants came up in support, and as soon as their R.M.Os. had formed Aid Posts they got in touch with our Bearer Posts. Evacuation of our own wounded continued smoothly.

H.Q. 73 F.A.,
9/6/17, 9 a.m.

John Cunningham
Lieut-Colonel R.A.M.C.,
O.C. 73 Field Ambulance.

DIAGRAM SHOWING LINES OF EVACUATION BETWEEN
REGIMENTAL AID POSTS & DRESSING STATIONS, ETC.

73rd F.A.
June 1917.

(App. C.)

ENEMY FRONT LINE TRENCHES

1 R.A.P. I.32.d.33.
2 R.A.P. I.32.c.505.
3 R.A.P. O.1.6.7.9.
4 R.A.P. O.1.6.26.

VOORMEZEELE
Collecting Post.

MIDDLESEX LANE

CAFÉ BELGE

OVERLAND ROUTE

C.C.P.

DICKEBUSCH LAKE

DICKEBUSCH H.2.d.3.1.
A.D.S.

BRANDHOEK

M.D.S. for L.W.

M.D.S. for S.W.

OUDERDOM G.20.a.5.2.
H.Q. F.A.

M.b.a.8.8.

A.D.M.S.
RENINGHELST

App. C.
73rd F.A.
June 1917.

R.A.P.s will be formed by M.Os. of the Battns. 24th Division. Pearson Division attached to Brigades will carry from these R.A.P.s to R.A.P.s of 41st Divn. where the wounded of the 24th Divn. will be taken over by the 41st Divn.

COMMITTEE FOR THE
MEDICAL HISTORY OF THE WAR
Date   10 SEP. 1917

No. 73. 7.a.

Army Form C. 2118.

WAR DIARY
or
INTELLIGENCE SUMMARY

73 Field Ambulance

July 1917   Page 1

Place	Date	Hour	Summary of Events and Information	Remarks and references to Appendices
R2289	1-7-17		General Routine- All the divisions were in training area - A. McN. & 2 O.R. proceed with the R.E. & R.A. to open towels Medical Inspection Room.	Operation Order—attached
"	2-7-17		4 Cars proceed to Division H.Q. miles away with 2 S. men fit for duty & one to return tomorrow with similar number for D.R.S. - To be a daily proceedure while Division is in Rest.	
R2289	10-7-17		Nothing of importance to note - Usual routine of a D.R.S.	
	16-7-17		Lieuts returned from Short Cercle- Lts Schell & Raby returned.	
	24-7-17		Nothing of importance to note - Usual routine of a D.R.S.	
	25-7-17		Wounded bodies proceed to 72 F.A. & large plain training station.	
	26-7-17		Remainder of Bearers & Cookers went forward - See attached orders.	
	31-7-17		The work of D.R.S. has continued with one small hiatus. A few wounded (mostly shell) were admitted today. [signature]	

OPERATION ORDER – 73rd FIELD AMBULANCE.

1. Headquarters "A" TENT SUB-DIVISION and "A" BEARER SUB-DIVISION (minus those required to bring "B" and "C" up to full strength) will remain at R.M.a.S.P. (Sheet 27) as a Divisional Rest Station.

2. "B" TENT SUB-DIVISION AND "C" TENT SUB-DIVISION under CAPTAIN WEIGALL will report to LIEUT-COL. D.P.PUDDICOMB, D.S.O., R.A.M.C. for duty at the CORPS MAIN DRESSING STATION FOR LIGHTLY WOUNDED. Date to be notified later.

3. "B" and "C" BEARER SUB-DIVISIONS, under CAPTAIN BRISCO, will evacuate the casualties of the 73rd Infantry Brigade from the Regimental Aid Posts backwards, under the orders of the Officer Commanding 72nd Field Ambulance. (See extracts from A.D.M.S. 24th Division, Medical Arrangements).

    CAPTAIN BRISCO will detail two reliable runners, who will wear red bands on the left fore-arm, to the Regimental Medical Officer of each Battalion of the Brigade.

    A holding party of Six Other Ranks under L/Cpl. WEBB, by permission of A.D.M.S. 38th Division, will proceed to WOODCOTE HOUSE on the 23rd instant, which is to be used in the events of the Light Railway between LARCH WOOD and LOCK 8 being disorganised.

    CAPTAIN BRISCO and 20 Other Ranks will report to Officer Commanding 72nd Field Ambulance on the 24th instant to learn the line of evacuation. The remainder of "B" and "C" Bearer Sub-divisions will report to Officer Commanding 72nd Field Ambulance on the evening of the 25th instant.

4. Sergt. MUSTABT with one Limber and one Water Cart will report to Officer Commanding 72nd Field Ambulance on the night of the 25th instant, to arrange for the distribution of rations to the personnel of the 73rd Field Ambulance.

EXTRACTS FROM A.D.M.S. 24th Division, MEDICAL ARRANGEMENTS. 784/7/20 dated 22/7/17.

EVACUATION TO REGIMENTAL AID POSTS.

Evacuation to R.A.Posts is to be carried out by Regimental Stretcher Bearers, augmented by a party to be detailed by O.C. Unit before the action commences. If this is still inadequate, application is to be made by O.C. Unit to Brigade Headquarters, and if the latter is unable to cope with the situation, application will be made to Divl.H'qrs."A" for further assistance.

EVACUATION FROM REGIMENTAL AID POSTS TO DIVISIONAL COLLECTING Post – Larch Wood.

This will be done by Hand Carry. The Bearer Divisions of the Field Ambulances will be responsible for the evacuation of the Wounded of their respective Brigades to LARCH WOOD. They will work under the orders of the Officer Commanding 72nd Field Ambulance, who will decide where they are to be stationed and will arrange for a reserve of bearers to be kept for the purposes of relief.

EVACUATION FROM LARCH WOOD TO LOCK 8.

This will be by Light Railway. O.C.72 Field Ambulance will detail sufficient bearers from those held in reserve to work the trolleys on this line, these bearers will be assisted by the Divisional Band, who will report to O.C. 72 Field Amb. on Y day.

The Corps has supplied 15 trolleys to work between LARCH WOOD and LOCK 8.

Ambulance Cars will be used if possible on the cross-country track via Spoil Bank, Chester Farm, Chapelle Farm & Jackson's Dump.

R.A.M.C.
OFFICER COMMANDING
73rd FIELD AMB.

140/264

No 73. 7.a.

Aug 17

COMMITTEE FOR THE
MEDICAL HISTORY OF THE WAR
Date -1 OCT.1917

WAR DIARY or INTELLIGENCE SUMMARY

Army Form C. 2118.

13th Field Ambulance

August 1914

Page 1.

Place	Date	Hour	Summary of Events and Information	Remarks and references to Appendices
Rd 089	1-8-14		Very wet weather. 39 wounded admitted.	
"	2-8-14		General tendency of D.R.S. [but may start] having to number of sick and lightly wounded coming in. Owing to wet weather great difficulty in getting the patients clothing dried. Visited O.J. & arranged for supply of clothing for those patients who come in deficient. Captain Goodwin returns Regt. Service in gaols here. 24 wounded.	
"	3-8-14		Weather still very wet & difficulty of drying clothing maximum. "Sick List" cases have started but very slight.	
"	4-8-6		Usual routine of a D.R.S. continues. Weather still very unsettled but in any interval clean dry clothing dry. Too men outfit for those who remain deficient. The "sick list" cases are now diminishing. Have been very full amongst over 100 coming a day— Improvements continues daily & at present	
"	20-8-14		Usual routine of a D.R.S. Special work with help of R.E. on storm drainage & roads	

Army Form C. 2118.

WAR DIARY
or
INTELLIGENCE SUMMARY

(Erase heading not required.)

13" Field Ambulance August 1914   Page 11

Place	Date	Hour	Summary of Events and Information	Remarks and references to Appendices
R2A89	31-8-14		Usual routine of a F.A.S. Many improvements to the cards since the beginning of the month - during the month 1750 patients have been admitted and 998 returned to duty - have sent in plans for turning this F.A.S. into a hutted hospital to meet the requirements of winter.	

J. Cunningham
Lt. Col.
Oct 13" g.A.

140/2438

No. 73. 7.a.

COMMITTEE FOR THE
MEDICAL HISTORY OF THE WAR
Date — 5 NOV. 1917

WAR DIARY or INTELLIGENCE SUMMARY

Army Form C. 2118.

73rd Field Ambulance

September 1917

Vol 25

Place	Date	Hour	Summary of Events and Information	Remarks and references to Appendices
In the Field	1/9/17 – 3/9/17		General Routine of D.R.S.	
R.A.P.	4/9/17		General Routine. Capt C.A. Brisco R.A.M.C. awarded the Military Cross.	
	5/9/17		General Routine. 5 P.B. men reported for duty as A.S.C. H.T. and taken on the strength.	
	6/9/17		General Routine. 5 A.S.C. H.T. proceeded to M.T.'s Base Depot. Have two reinforcements R.A.M.C. reported for duty taken on the strength.	
	7/9/17		General Routine. A.D.M.S. 24th Division visited D.R.S. Weather fine.	
	8/9/17		General Routine. D.D.M.S. & Capt x-visited D.R.S. 1 N.C.O. + 10 men proceeded to forward area to build Regimental Aid Posts. 2nd Lieut Godmann O.M. M.D.R.C. (U.S.A) attached for duty.	
	9-11/9/17		General Routine D.R.S.	
	12/9/17		Movement Orders received also orders to evacuate & return to duty all 24th Div D.R.S cases 61 cases from 23rd Div admitted.	
	13/9/17		General Routine. Capt R.W. Cushing R.A.M.C.T.F. proceeded to 9th E. Surrey Regt for temporary duty. Lt. Col. J.N. Crimshaw returns from leave.	
Doulieu	15.9.17		The F.A. travelled to Doulieu – Weather fine – No loss etc. –	
"	16-9-17 – 20-9		Rest area – Equipment parades + lodgings on the farm when billeted –	

Army Form C. 2118.

13° Field Ambulance

WAR DIARY
or
INTELLIGENCE SUMMARY
(Erase heading not required.)

Sheet 57 C
Sheet 62 C
September 1919 Page 11

Place	Date	Hour	Summary of Events and Information	Remarks and references to Appendices
Sheet 57-C O.21.b.26	21-9-19		Marched at 2 A.M. & entrained at BAPAUME and marched to camp here.	
"	22-9-19		Except for collection of Brigade sick no event & hardly anything of importance to note.	
"	23-9-19			
Lcq/Estreé	24-9-19		Left at 9 & marched to Lcq/Estreé. Many sick collected on March. O.C. & 2 Lt. visited 102 & 103 F.A. with a view of taking over Main dressing station and advanced posts.	
BERNES	25-9-19		Marched to BERNES in fine weather. Billeted till 102 F.A. Captain Russlin and a small party proceeds to A.D.S. Templeux and later marched to Jeancourt.	
"	26-9-19		Took over Main dressing station at 12 noon. Sadrin went to the A.D.S.	
"	27-9-19		Lift equipment to relieve 102. J.A. General routine. Visited the D.S. & went round the R.A.P.'s from which we evacuate. Arrange for far to remain at H.Q. 73° Brigade for night work which the relieve the Stewart of a lot of work.	

WAR DIARY or INTELLIGENCE SUMMARY

1/3 Field Ambulance Map 62c September 1917 Page III

Place	Date	Hour	Summary of Events and Information	Remarks and references to Appendices
BERNES	28-9-17 / 29-9-17		General Routine of a Main Dressing station with A.D.S.	Evacuation scheme attached - Diagramatic.
"	30-9-17		Hands over the site at JEANCOURT to 1/4 F.A. + all the men then returned to H.Q. All cases though JEANCOURT are however still evacuated through H.Q. of this unit.	

J M Cunningham
Lt Col
O.C. 1/3 F.A.

app I

73rd. FIELD AMBULANCE.

OPERATION ORDER.

(1) The sick of the Brigade will be collected by ambulance cars at 8.30 a.m. prompt on the 20th. inst. Any such sick will be evacuated from Headquarters by horse ambulance.

(2) The Divisional ambulance cars, under Capt. Weigall, will rendezvous at MERRIS on MERRIS-STRAZEELE Road at 10 a.m. on the 20th. inst.

The column will proceed to the THIRD ARMY AREA, reporting on arrival to the Town Major, BAPAUME.

Route:- AIRE-ST.POL-DOULLENS-ALBERT.

The head of the column will not be South of AIRE before 11 a.m.

Two days rations will be carried.

(3) An advance party consisting of Sgt. Jackson, Cpl. Lemon, L/Cpl. Atkins, Ptes. Churchill, Cassidy, and Henderson, will travel on the train of the 2nd. Leinster Regiment, which leaves BAILLEUL (Main Station) at 10.28 a.m. on the 20th. inst.

This party will report to the Brigade representative at the entraining station at 9.28 a.m. Two days rations will be carried.

Capt. Weigall will get in touch with this party on arrival at their destination, and will be the Officer in charge.

(4) The Field Ambulance will parade at 2 a.m. on the morning of the 21st. inst., ready to move off. "C" Section will parade at their own billets, and join the remainder of the column at the "T" road near Headquarters.

Haversack rations will be carried.

JohnCunningham
Lieut.Col.R.A.M.C.,
Commanding 73rd.Fld.Ambce.

19.9.17.

App. II

75th FIELD AMBULANCE.

OPERATION ORDER.

1. 75rd Field Ambulance will parade at 9.45am under Captain Rudkin, and be at Road Junction O.19.d.5.2. at 10.15am ready to march to HAUT-ALLAINES.

2. Route - ROCQUIGNY - MANANCOURT - MOISLAINS -

3. 73rd Infantry Brigade Operation Order No.125 will be strictly adhered to.

4. One Horse Ambulance will report to the M.O., 7th Northants 8.30
       do.   do.   do. M.O., 9th R.Sussex. 8.45
   One Sunbeam Car do.   do. M.O. 13th Middlesex, 9.0
       do.   do.   do. M.O. 2nd Leinsters, 9.30
   for duty on the march. On completion of the march they will return to H.Q., 75rd Fd.Amb.

5. 76th Field Ambulance is arranging for a car to accompany the 12th Royal Fusiliers.

6. A motor cyclist will visit the Medical Inspection Rooms of the various Battalions by 8.30am to enquire the number of sick, if any, requiring evacuation. Cars will then be detailed as required.

7. Orders for the advance party under Captain Weigall, who will take over billets from Staff Captain, will be issued separately.

Lieut.Col. R.A.M.C.
Commanding 75rd Field Ambulance

22/2/17.

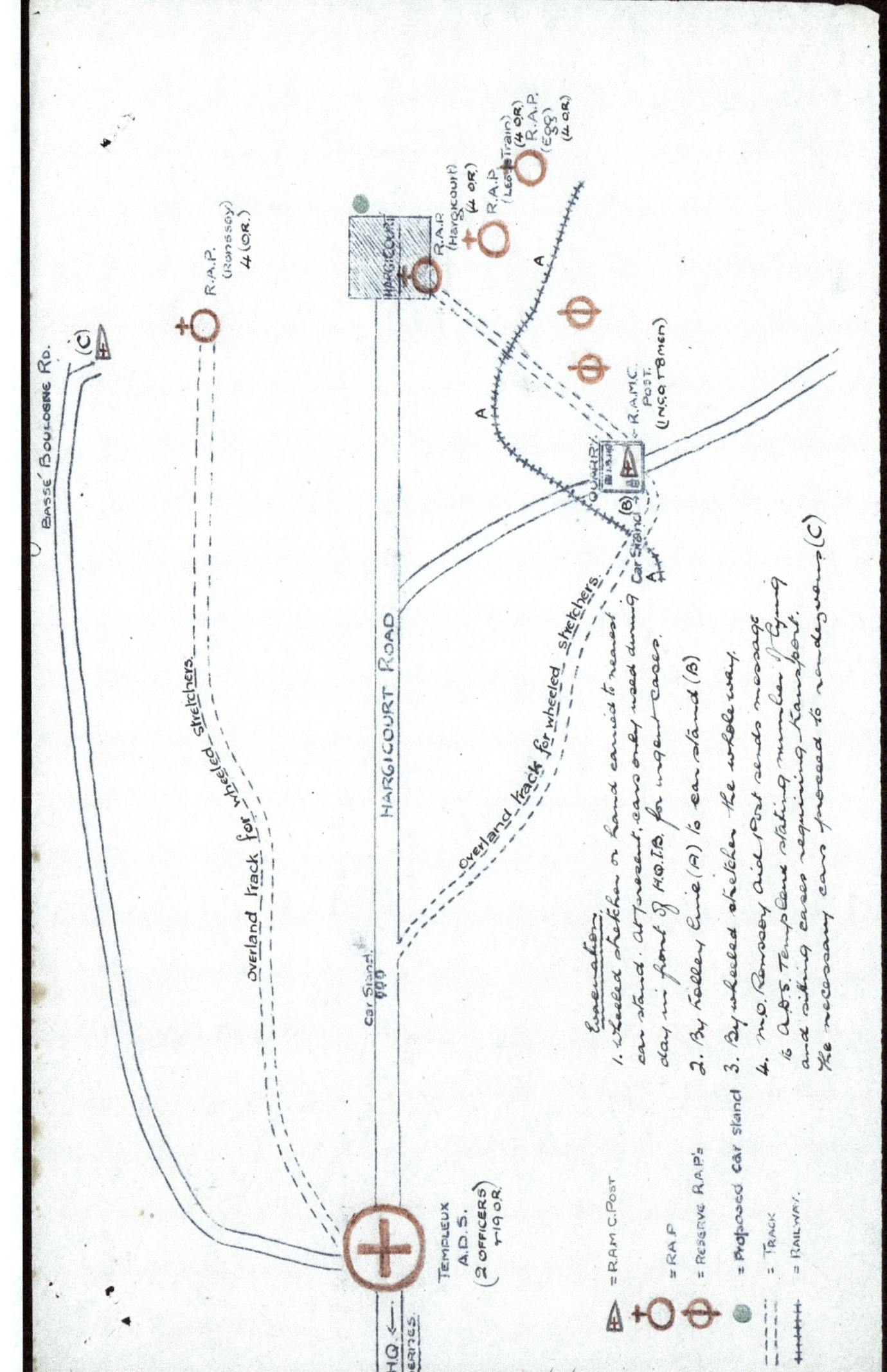

Contributions 16

Oct. 1917

140/499

9/1/26

War Diary
73rd Field Ambulance
1st O.Later
1917

COMMITTEE FOR THE
MEDICAL HISTORY OF THE WAR
Date — 8 DEC. 1917

Army Form C. 2118.

WAR DIARY
or
INTELLIGENCE SUMMARY

73rd Field Ambulance

Page 1

October 1917

(Erase heading not required.)

Instructions regarding War Diaries and Intelligence Summaries are contained in F. S. Regs., Part II. and the Staff Manual respectively. Title Pages will be prepared in manuscript.

Place	Date	Hour	Summary of Events and Information	Remarks and references to Appendices
BERNES	1-10-17		Visited A.D.S. Templeux + the Old posts on left of line – Usual routine –	
"	2-10-17		Usual routine – Nil to note –	
"	3-10-17		A.&.M.S. visited the A.D.S at Templeux and the R.A.P. of the Sussex, Northants +	
"	4-10-17		Cat dennys. Construction work at H.Q. Programme well also at A.D.S.	
"	5-10-17		Usual routine – Construction programme + also visited Kitchen stables –	
"	6-10-17			
"	7-10-17		Potamis Sighz + broken aspects for duty – The Battery line has too few Offrs. to HARGICOURT so all the R.A.P.s except the one on left on connected ref or occupied by Inds. – See no diagram to conversation –	
"	8-10-17		Lt. GOUCHMAN proceeded to 2nd LEINSTER Regt. for duty – Arranged that car should run to base Boulogne by cases from left R.A.P. when sent for by orderly or through Brigade Telephone –	
"	10-10-17		Visited the R.A.P.s and A.D.s – Weather fine but have again started – Dr. H.Q. hand torture + construction	

WAR DIARY or INTELLIGENCE SUMMARY

Army Form C. 2118.

43° Field Ambulance October 1917 Page II

Place	Date	Hour	Summary of Events and Information	Remarks and references to Appendices
BERNES	11-10-17		G.O.C. of division inspects the Field Ambulance	
"	12-10-17		Usual routine. Evacuation not progressing well in front & back area.	
"	13-10-17		Parade in morning for Inspection of medals by the Corps Commander in afternoon. Grand Rabbi U.S.A. visited the B.A.	
"	14-10-17 15-10-17		Usual routine – nil of importance.	
"	16-10-17		Visited the left section of the line with M.O. Middlesex & arranged for cars to go further side the road for some cases.	
"	17-10-17		13. I.B. have gone to new quarters & have held our some day also. Visits R.A.M.C. Post to increase our accommodation & make a Stored unpoli huts given to extricate before transferring from Trolley System to cars.	
			Bearer trainees – Stretcher continues [...] in 3 feet.	

WAR DIARY or INTELLIGENCE SUMMARY

Army Form C. 2118.

73ʳᵈ Field Ambulance

October 1917

Page II

Place	Date	Hour	Summary of Events and Information	Remarks and references to Appendices
BERNES	21-10-17		Major [?] Lawrence visited the F.A.	
"	22-10-17		Visited all the Fwd Ones - Evacuation scheme early but very few cases.	
"	23-10-17		R.B.M.S. visited the A.D.S. TINCPLEUX and ROISEL and Main dressing station.	
"	27-10-17		Nothing of importance to note - Usual routine - hardly any had.	
"	31-10-17		Usual routine of a quiet sector of front line. There has been nothing of importance to note this month - Instruction work has gone on apace in front and back area + Left the A.D.S. & Main dressing station and dealt with large numbers of wounded should the necessity arise. The evacuation system is however at last to all except F.I. cars now 80 visits made at night made to inform evidence of the border.	

Signed [illegible]
Lt. [?]
O.C. 73ʳᵈ F.A.

SECRET.

WAR DIARY.

73rd FIELD AMBULANCE

From November to November 30th

1917.

COMMITTEE FOR THE
MEDICAL HISTORY OF THE WAR
Date 17 JAN. 1918

WAR DIARY or INTELLIGENCE SUMMARY

Army Form G. 2118.

93rd Field Ambulance

November 1919 Map 62c.

Place	Date	Hour	Summary of Events and Information	Remarks and references to Appendices
BERNES	1-11-19		General routine. Nothing important to note.	
"	2-11-19			
"	3-11-19			
"	4-11-19		Had all C.R.E. to H.Q. of 12th Shopwards to discuss the making of a new A.D.S. site and to visit in case of advance on a big attack.	
"	6-11-19		With D.R.E. and A.D.M.S. visited L.S.R.1 + decided to have an A.D.S. there — 40 O.R. details from the 2 ambulances of the division are working at it under the supervision of the D.R.E. Brigade + have special arrangements in case of casualties during the repels raid — No casualties. Men were brought through from because of heavy shelling on Beauvin Battalion areas.	
"	9-11-19		The Methods raided the enemy trenches. No casualties to the wire Beauvin + Caen returned to H.Q. last night.	
"	10-11-19			
"	11-11-19		Usual routine. Nothing of importance to note.	
"	12-11-19		The G.O.C. visits Hospital. Officers mess routine —	
"	14-11-19		Visits Brigade + Implement. Also all RAPs on this front + the new A.D.S. in town of Destruction at WARGICOURT. Have general arrangements for RAPs + possible affmeri	

2449 Wt. W14957/M90 750,000 1/16 J.B.C. & A. Forms/C.2118/12.

Army Form C. 2118.

Page II
Map 62 c

93rd Field Ambulance **WAR DIARY** or **INTELLIGENCE SUMMARY**

November 1917

(Erase heading not required.)

Place	Date	Hour	Summary of Events and Information	Remarks and references to Appendices
BERNES	15th 16/11/17 17		Usual Routine – Nothing of importance to note –	
"	18/11/17		Hostilities Patrol withdrawn from Front area – one N.C.O. + 2 nursing orderlies lent to 5 F.As for temporary duty – visits 72nd + 73rd Brigade + arrangements for possible future operations –	
"	19/11/17		Bearers to all R.A.Ps + A.D.S. Ambulance to but remain tomorrow morning early –	
"	20/11/17		2 Brick admissions today – No difficulty with Evacuations –	
"	21/11/17 22/11/17 23/11/17		Usual Routine – Nil of importance to note –	
"	24/11/17		All bearers have again withdrawn to H.Q. Nothing else to note	

Army Form C. 2118.

Page iii

42ⁿᵈ Field Ambulance

WAR DIARY
or
INTELLIGENCE SUMMARY.
(Erase heading not required.)

November 1917

Map 62c

Place	Date	Hour	Summary of Events and Information	Remarks and references to Appendices
BERNES	25/11/17 26/11/17 27/11/17		Normal routine. Nothing of importance to note.	
BERNES	28/11/17		Received movement orders to proceed to HAUT ALLAINES area and take the Brigade on ReLief. Visited Brigade & arranged for the hand-over.	
BERNES	29/11/17		All movement orders cancelled & orders to stand by received & enemy attack on our Left. Visited Brigade & in view of possible attack on our front specially the left took up transverse Beams also re-establish the Post at HARDY BANK. Visited Templeux A.Ds. & the Sunken Road.	
BERNES	30/11/17		9th Stationary Hy. Draw-els several wounded Indiain-Yanks Brigade & A.Ds. Nothing further has happened up to date.	

JM Cunningham
Lt Col
O.C. 1/3 FA

Confidential

73rd Field Ambulance. R.A.M.C

War Diary for the month of December, 17.

Volume 28.

Army Form C. 2118.

42 - Field Ambulance

WAR DIARY
or
INTELLIGENCE SUMMARY.
(Erase heading not required.)

December 1919
Map 62.
Page 1.

Place	Date	Hour	Summary of Events and Information	Remarks and references to Appendices
BERNES	1-12-19 / 2-12-19		Usual routine - Still standing bye - Keeping the teams up at Templeux. Weather fine + frosty.	
"	3-12-19		Visits the Brigade + Templeux A.D.S. Nothing important except Raids to direct to Kilnown the wbs cars and parade lent to H.Q. + to W. then me weekly at Hagwin. Placed a motor cycle at disposal of M.O. i/c A.D.S.	
"	4-12-19		1 Officer + 6 O.R. + 2 H/tons Ambulances of 4th Cavalry Fd. details for A.D.S. Templeux to work with this unit. Nothing else of importance to note.	
"	6-12-19		Visits Brigade - then A.D.S. Templeux + the R.A.P.s of the 72" + 73". Brigade wished to arrange for Raid which our troops from tonight - Sent up extra bearers + equipment also cars to Templeux - D.D.M.S. visits unit.	
"	7-12-19		Extra bearers returned to H.Q. Two of the raids did not come off - Very few casualties from them.	
"	8-12-19		11/4 F.A. took over Roisel + the Con. departnent at BERNES on billets. Nothing else of importance to note.	

43rd Field Ambulance

WAR DIARY **December 1919**
or
INTELLIGENCE SUMMARY. Map 62c
(Erase heading not required.)

Army Form C. 2118.

Page iii

Place	Date	Hour	Summary of Events and Information	Remarks and references to Appendices
BECOURT	9-12-19		General routine — Weather fine very wet.	
"	10-12-19		Lt. Hunter proceeds to 2nd Leinsters for duty — Visits the ADS + arranges for a raid on 43rd Brigade front. Weather fine again.	
"	11-12-19		Usual routine — AD to HA.	
"	12-12-19		No casualties at all from last night raid. B.D.M.S. Lovely order with Lt. Sergeant — raider shells — had to stop + arranged several minor points. S.D.S.1 + arranged several minor points. It temporarily evacuated.	
"	16-12-19		Usual routine. Weather fine. Lt. Shannon + Lt. Peck, M.S.C.A. attached for duty + instruction - Visits ADS, Templeux + Lt. Sqte of R.E. have arranged to strengthen 1 leaves of the penetrate shelling in Naylorton.	
"	17-12-19		ADSS his P.B. Board at top Heavy snowstorm and snowcarts which camp attempting journey has to be dug out of snowdrifts + returns to HQ.	
	18-12-19		General routine — Roads again fit for transport line + goods.	

2353 Wt. W25+/1452 700,000 5/15 D.D.&L. A.D.S.S./Form/C2118.

WAR DIARY

43rd Field Ambulance

December 1917

Map 62

Page III

Place	Date	Hour	Summary of Events and Information	Remarks and references to Appendices
BERNES	19.12.17		1 M.O. + 20 O.R. of 2 Fd. Amb. to have taken over the R.A.P. at E.Q.R. + post at Brevain from us. They evacuate into A.D.S. Templeux as before. Visited the A.D.S. + posts.	
"	23.12.17		Usual routine. Many sick admissions at Brevain. Steady improvement at Templeux + strengthening of Brevain from men previously absent.	
"	25.12.17		Visited A.D.S. + all the posts with Lieut. Sievier. The sick rate remains high. Weather fine but very cold.	
"	26.12.17 27.12.17 28.12.17		Usual routine. Nil of importance.	
"	29.12.17		A.D.M.S. visited H.Q. Weather still fine but very cold.	
"	31.12.17		The Cavalry posts relieved by a similar number. Otherwise usual routine.	

J.H.J. Munro(?) Lt Col
OC 43 F.A.

Confidential

73rd Field Ambulance

War Diary for the month of January, 1918.

WAR DIARY or INTELLIGENCE SUMMARY

Army Form C.2118

143rd Field Ambulance

January 1918

Page I   Map 62.

Place	Date	Hour	Summary of Events and Information	Remarks and references to Appendices
BERNES	1-1-18		D.D.M.S. Corps inspected main Dressing Station. Special reference to the opening of a Gas treatment centre. Shells the occasion arise.	
"	2-1-18		Visits A.D.S. Templeux. Shed has been done to strengthen this place but it is not yet what clear proof + is extremely long walls - roofs of dug-outs again show the advisability of moving it.	
"			Naval stations. Nothing of importance to date. Thaw set in followed by snow storms after two days of frost.	
"	8-1-18		B. Peak proceeded to 7th Battalion to 7th Battalion for temporary duty. Snow again fell heavily followed by frost.	
"	10-1-18		Heavy shelling again at Templeux. One of the huts was set on fire + burnt value. Main discussed the question of evacuating Templeux. The A.D.M.S. is to consult with the C.R.E.	

WAR DIARY
INTELLIGENCE SUMMARY

23- FA.   January 1918   Army Form C.2
Page II   Map 62C

Place	Date	Hour	Summary of Events and Information	Remarks and references to Appendices
BERNES	11-1-18		Usual routine – Std of indigenous.	
"	12-1-18		Severe weather – Stamped in a number of sick returned – Made out a full scheme for sanitation & treatment of scared cases in case of a large gas attack & (generally) it to A.D.M.S.	
"	13-1-18		It has been decided to make a dump dug out under the sunken portion of trenches as extra sick front accommodation. Extra men sent up to help in this. Later to walk a hurry H.Q. Let the site be properly in the last known Brigade H.Q. Finally decided on by R.E.	
"	14-1-18		Usual routine. Consulting surgeon S.Army visited D.M.D.S. & gave a lecture on S.A. work.	
"	15-1-18		Hand over to Capt. Hergath Rawn prior to going on leave	

[signature]

Army Form C.

73rd F.A.

WAR DIARY or INTELLIGENCE SUMMARY.

January 1918

Map 62.c.

Instructions regarding War Diaries and Intelligence Summaries are contained in F.S. Regs., Part II. and the Staff Manual respectively. Title pages will be prepared in manuscript. Page iii

Place	Date	Hour	Summary of Events and Information	Remarks and references to Appendices
BERNES	16/1/18		General routine. Very heavy weather. Tents & marquees blown down.	
"	17/1/18		Capt. Ruchin M.C. relieved Capt. Brown M.C. at A.D.S.	
"	18/1/18		Work proceeding on Corpn. Gas Centre. Construction of baths & re-erection of marquees.	
"	19/1/18		Visited Templeuve. Work proceeding slowly on dugout owing to difficulty with the wet overhead. Shelling has been very heavy here recently, many 5.9 and 8.2" being used in the immediate vicinity of A.D.S. Settled on proposed new site of A.D.S. with Capt. Ruchin M.C.	
"	20/1/18		Visited A.D.M.S. and obtained his sanction for construction of new A.D.S. No. 2 Cav. F.A. relieved No. 4 Cav. F.A. in the forward area.	
"	21/1/18		General routine. Nothing of importance to note.	
"	22/1/18		"	
"	23/1/18		"	
"	24/1/18		A.D.M.S. 4 Cav. Div. visited M.D.S. to arrange check the Indian (then on on 27/1/18	
"	25/1/18		General routine	
"	26/1/18		"	

Army Form C. 2118

73 Fd Amb

WAR DIARY
or
INTELLIGENCE SUMMARY.

January 1918 Map 62.C

Page iv

(Erase heading not required.)

Place	Date	Hour	Summary of Events and Information	Remarks and references to Appendices
BERNES	27/1/18		Visited Templeux A.D.S. Went forward actually on road and offered greater shelter. Fld that retained No 2 Fld Amb is favour area. Gas centre evacuated by 74th Fld Amb.	
	28/1/18		Visited D.M.S. re new A.D.S, the proposed site of which has been changed by the Corps. Capt Brown M.C. relieves Capt Ruchin M.C. at the A.D.S. Fine weather a hostile bombing at night	
	29 30 31	1.18 3.05	Usual routine. Nothing of importance to note	

Aweigned Capt RAMC

<u>Confidential</u>

<u>73rd Field Ambulance</u>

War Diary for the month of February, 1918.

Army Form C.

73rd Fld Amb. WAR DIARY February 1918
or
INTELLIGENCE SUMMARY. Map 62 c
Page 1
(Erase heading not required.)

Place	Date	Hour	Summary of Events and Information	Remarks and references to Appendices
BERNES	1/2/18		Visited Templeuve A.D.S. & fwds	
"	2/2/18		Went round on Corps Gas Centre	
"	3/2/18		Lieut Dalles reported for temporary duty. Capt. Ruchin M.C. relieved	
			Capt Brown M.C. at A.D.S	
"	4/2/18		Ordinary routine	
"	5/2/18		Lieut B - the relieved Capt Ruchin M.C. at A.D.S	
			D.M.S. visited M.D.S and Corps Gas Centre	
"	6/2/18		Visited A.D.M.S.	
"	7/2/18		A.D.M.S. visited M.D.S.	
"	8/2/18		Visited Templeuve - new A.D.S. site. The three entrance dugs	
"	9/2/18		here are now nearly completed	
"	10/2/18		Ordinary routine	
"	11/2/18			
"	12/2/18		Visited both A.D.S.s - with D.A.D.M.S.	
"	13/2/18		Ordinary routine	
"	14/2/18		A.D.M.S. visited M.D.S. Relieved forward of Seclehit Folo Hut in forward area	

WAR DIARY
INTELLIGENCE SUMMARY

737 FM Unit
February 1918
Part II
M of 62 c

Place	Date	Hour	Summary of Events and Information	Remarks and references to Appendices
BERNES	15/2/18		Inspected open country between HESBECOURT and HARGICOURT with reference to elaborate methods of execution from front area in event of movement of dummy return in colliery H and Lient Col Cunningham returned from leave. J.H.H Cunningham Lt Col	
	16/2/18		Usual routine. Visited the A.D.S. template. In advance that very satisfactory — arranged that steps should be taken immediately to put this right. A.D.Vehicle	
	21/2/18		Proceeded to No 32 I.C.C. + struck off the strength. A.D.V.S. 66th Division visited the Van drawing stations and called limited Record Office + the San centre with a view of taking it over in new Station. Visited the new bleaching oven and arranged run of details of same. Also visited Brigade H.Q.	
	22/2/18		Usual routine. Inspection of villages + by Corps Commander. Directed the other works parades under Captain Baird.	
	25/2/18		Left on ½ of last leave. F.A. with A.D.S. and all the journey will and little a little of loading me on Mark 2" before proceeding to Kent and a —	

73rd Field Ambulance WAR DIARY or INTELLIGENCE SUMMARY.

January 1918 Map 62c
Page iii

Place	Date	Hour	Summary of Events and Information	Remarks and references to Appendices
BERNES	27/2/18		Usual routine. An advanced party of 1 Officer and 24 ORs proceed to Templeux + 1 Officer and 21 ORs to Bernes from 2/3 East Lancs. FA.	
"	28/1/18		Usual routine. A temporary number to be drawn forty of 2/3 East Lancs. of this unit returned to H.Q. Capt. Kendall + 2 OR proceed to Le PARACLET as an advance party.	

J.S.M. Cunningham
Lt. Col. OC 73. FA.

WAR DIARY
(ORIGINAL)

73rd FIELD AMBULANCE

MARCH 1918

Army Form C. 2118.

73rd Field Ambulance

WAR DIARY or INTELLIGENCE SUMMARY

Instructions regarding War Diaries and Intelligence Summaries are contained in F.S. Regs., Part II and the Staff Manual respectively. Title Pages will be prepared in manuscript.

Month and Year: March 1918

Map — AMIENS (Sheet 17)

Sheet 1.

Place	Date 1918	Hour	Summary of Events and Information	Remarks and references to Appendices
	March 1.		General routine. Move into rest area cancelled. Orders to be ready to move out at short notice.	
	2		Handed over to 2/3 East Lancs. F. Amb. This unit billeted with them.	
	3-12.		Training according to attached programme, and waiting orders to move. Advance party proceeded to Trefcon.	
	12		Moved to Trefcon and took over site from 6th Cav. F. Amb.	
	13		General routine. Improving camp, increasing accommodation for patients.	
	14–19		General routine. DDMS, XIX Corps & ADMS 24 Div: inspected camp.	
	20		Visited Divisional Baths Vraignes to arrange for its conversion into "Mustard Gas" Centre in case of need. Party of 20 picked to stand by for this purpose.	
	21		German offensive started early this morning. All ambulance standing to and party sent to Vraignes Gas Centre. Just cars for duty at Control Post. Received orders to move at 3am to St Emer and arrived at dawn. Standing by all day for further orders. At 11pm received orders to be across the Bridge Head at St Erie before dawn and assemble at Marchelpot.	
	22		Arrived at Marchelpot at dawn. At 11 am sent up cars and a bearer sub-division under Capt Brisco to the Bridge heads at St Fany and St Even to evacuate wounded of retiring Brigades after the bridge had been blown up, this bearer subdivision kept in touch with Brigades and HQ evacuated down to Marchelpot where an Advanced Dressing Station was formed. Some cases were evacuated direct on to the train at the adjoining C.C.S. which was closing down, others were sent by car to Villers Bretonneux.	
	23		The transport was sent to Hallu early in the afternoon. A party of the 8th Division arrived at 10.30pm and took over the Advanced Dressing Station, after which the party rejoined the transport at Hallu, except for the bearer sub-division	

Army Form C. 2118.

WAR DIARY
or
INTELLIGENCE SUMMARY

73rd Field Ambulance Sheet 3

(Erase heading not required.)

MAP — AMIENS (Sheet 17).

Place	Date 1918	Hour	Summary of Events and Information	Remarks and references to Appendices
	March 28		Sent cases in own cars to transport lines at Demuin, where a temporary dressing station was opened by Captain Rudkin, M.C. Managed to clear by 1 pm and all further cases were directed straight to Demuin. Cleared out of Bayzee at 2.15 pm en route for Demuin, but on the road got orders to proceed to Thiennes where the transport had gone some hours previously. Captain Rudkin stayed on with wounded at Demuin until all had been evacuated later in the evening the whole unit was ordered to Rouvrel but remained closed, arriving about 10 pm.	
	29		Received orders 11 am to concentrate the Field Ambulances at St Sauflieu. A long march much delayed by transport through alley — Jumel — Oresmeaux.	
	30.		Received orders to stand by to move at a moment's notice.	
	31.		Nothing further to note.	

J W Cunningham
Lt Col
A/O 73. F.A.

73rd FIELD AMBULANCE.

WAR DIARY.
(ORIGINAL).

APRIL 1918.

VOLUME No. 32.

Army Form C. 2118.

"A" 93rd Field Ambulance

Map References
AMIENS. SHEET 17.
ABBEVILLE " 14
LENS " 11

SHEET 1.
WAR DIARY
or
INTELLIGENCE SUMMARY

APRIL 1918

(Erase heading not required.)

Instructions regarding War Diaries and Intelligence Summaries are contained in F.S. Regs., Part II. and the Staff Manual respectively. Title Pages will be prepared in manuscript.

Place	Date	Hour	Summary of Events and Information	Remarks and references to Appendices
SAINT SAUFLIEU	1/4/18 & 2/4/18		Headquarters unit at SAINT SAUFLIEU. Two bearer sub. divisions under Capt. Brisco proceeded to 74 F.A., A.D.S. at GOTTENOHY, together with all available Motor and Horse ambulances. Received orders to proceed to C.W.W. Post, Rue de la Porte Paris, AMIENS, in conjunction with 72 Field Ambulance. Left ST SAUFLIEU at 10 a.m. & arrived at AMIENS at 1.30 p.m. O.C. 72 F.A. in command of the post.	
AMIENS	4/4/18		27 bearers of Capt. Brisco's party attacked for duty to 73 F.A. (9 to each Battn). Capt. Brisco & remainder of bearer sub-division move with 74 F.A. to BOVES. Reserve bearers ready to move at short notice.	
	5/4/18		Took over the C.W.W. post from 72 F.A. about 10 p.m. Received orders re entraining for new area on 6th inst.	
	6/4/18		About 100 cases through C.W.W.P. up to 9 a.m. This unit relieved by 23rd Home Counties Field Ambulance at 9 a.m. Unit transport under O.C. Divn Trans. moved off at 7.30 p.m. for the ST. VALERY (SOMME) area. Headquarters, Nursing Sections and reserve bearers marched to SALEUX (entraining station) at 11.30 a.m. Capt. Brisco & bearer sub. division rejoin HQ.	
SALEUX			from 74 F.A. Unit stayed overnight at SALEUX.	

Army Form C. 2118.

SHEET 2.

77 Field Ambulance

WAR DIARY or INTELLIGENCE SUMMARY

(Erase heading not required.)

Title Pages APRIL 1918

Instructions regarding War Diaries and Intelligence Summaries are contained in F. S. Regs., Part II. and the Staff Manual respectively. Title Pages will be prepared in manuscript.

Place	Date	Hour	Summary of Events and Information	Remarks and references to Appendices
VALINES	7/4/18		Unit entrained at 5 p.m., and detrained at ST. VALERY about 8.30 p.m. Marched to VALINES, and arrived shortly after midnight.	
	8/4/18		Transport arrived about mid-day. The 27 bearers who were attached to 73 I.B. rejoin unit. Weather wet, consequently no routine except necessary fatigues. Arrangements made for collection at Brigade and 1st Aid Stick.	
	9/4/18 to 16/4/18		Mobilization equipment of the unit overhauled and unnecessary articles returned to Ordnance. Spare harness filled with Shell Dressings &c, and Medical Comforts. Equipment of personnel made up as far as possible. General routine with a few short route marches to break in new boots etc.	
	16/4/18		Orders received re move to First Army Area.	
	17/4/18		Unit marched off from VALINES at 11.30 a.m. & proceeded to WOINCOURT (entraining station). Entrained at 7.30 p.m.	
	18/4/18		Detrained at PERNES at 11 a.m. & marched to BEUGIN. Arrangements made for collection of Brigade Sick.	
BEUGIN	19/4/18 to 29/4/18		General Routine in rest area. Route marches, and declining drill with Gas Helmet training on alternate days continued. Bringing men's equipment up to date, also clearing up of transport, & re-adjustment of new ambulance equipment. The Field Ambulance inspected by D.D.M.S. Corps on 25th inst.	

2449 Wt. W14957/M90 750,000 1/16 J.B.C. & A. Forms/C.2118/12.

73rd Field Ambulance

Army Form C. 2118.

WAR DIARY
or
INTELLIGENCE SUMMARY
(Erase heading not required.)

March 1918

Map – AMIENS (Sheet 17)

Sheet 2.

Place	Date 1918	Hour	Summary of Events and Information	Remarks and references to Appendices
	March 24		Capt. Brisco and bearer sub-division reported HQ at Haillu at 9am. At 11am orders received that all transport was to go to Bayeux while the bearer and nursing divisions were to concentrate on Chilly and keep in touch with the 72nd and 75th Infantry Brigades at Haillu and Punchy respectively. Nothing further happened during the day.	
	25		Visited Brigades at 9am and learnt that they were going forward to the attack with the French. In consequence, brought up bearers to Punchy at 11am. Formed an advanced post with cars at cross roads near railway and of Advance Dressing Station at Haillu. At 2pm received orders to retire, also A.D.S. at Haillu shelled out. Opened one at Chilly which was also shelled out, so opened again at Maucourt. Had bearer posts and cars on the Punchy – Haillu & Chilly road bringing back wounded to Maucourt, and reserve bearers in dugouts at Chilly.	
	26		At 4am received orders to retire further. Took HQ and nursing Section to Rosieres and formed Advanced Dressing Station at Mehaucourt, with cars & bearer post on the Mehaucourt – Maucourt – Chilly road. At 9am had orders to retire to Bayeux and form a main Dressing Station there, with cars and bearers working along the Bayeux – Caix – Ouby road, in conjunction with 74 Field Ambulance. Main Dressing Station formed in old French hospital just outside Bayeux, and wounded came in continuously from the various Brigades. Some difficulty in getting them away owing to lack of MAC, cars and lorries	
	27		Main Dressing Station kept open at Bayeux and some arrangements for bringing wounded in. Still difficulty in getting them away, but with the help of some empty ammunition lorries managed to get over 100 walking wounded away to Villers – Bretoneux in charge of a sergeant, who eventually got them to the nearest C.C.S. In the evening the transports was ordered to Dennis.	

Army Form C. 2118.

Sheet 1

WAR DIARY
or
INTELLIGENCE SUMMARY

73rd Field Ambulance

(Erase heading not required.)

APRIL 1918

Instructions regarding War Diaries and Intelligence Summaries are contained in F. S. Regs., Part II. and the Staff Manual respectively. Title Pages will be prepared in manuscript.

Place	Date	Hour	Summary of Events and Information	Remarks and references to Appendices
BEUGIN	19/4/18 to 29/4/18		On 1st the Ambulance inspected by A.D.M.S., and the A.D.M.S., 2nd Division.	
FOSSE 10	30/4/18		Orders received to proceed to FOSSE 10. Left BEUGIN at 2.30 p.m. and arrived at FOSSE 10 at 6.30 p.m. Unit billeted with the 10th Canadian Field Ambce. An advance party of one Officer + 15 other ranks proceeded to the various aid posts in the sector.	

J. M. ——
Lieut. Col. R.A.M.C.
O.C. 73rd Field Ambulance

2449 Wt. W14957/M90 750,000 1/16 J.B.C. & A. Forms/C.2118/12.

73 FIELD AMBULANCE.

WAR DIARY.

MAY 1918.   VOLUME 33.

(ORIGINAL COPY)

WAR DIARY or INTELLIGENCE SUMMARY — Army Form C. 2118

73 Field Ambulance
Sheet No. 1
Map References: Sheets 44A + 44B
May 1918

Place	Date	Hour	Summary of Events and Information	Remarks and references to Appendices
FOSSE 10.	1/5/18		Took over H.Q. at Fosse 10, A.D.S's at Brig Lt Pierre & Fort Glatz. Relay Bath & Soap from No. 10 Canadian Field Ambulance. H.Q. and found area visited by A.D.M.S. all N.C.O's + men posted to their respective duties at the M.D.S. (H.Q.)	
	2/5/18 3/5/18 4/5/18		General Louber much work on hand in connection with improvements to the M.D.S. at Fosse 10. A number of our bearers relieved by parties from 7 F.A. visited front area with the A.D.M.S & discussed further schemes of evacuation.	
	5/5/18		H.Qr. inspected by D.O.C. & Subn. & the A.D.M.S.	
	7/5/18		D.D.M.S XVIII Corps & A.D.M.S 1st Div visited the M.D.S. and also the A.D.S. at Brit Lt Pierre. Received orders to establish a Gas Centre at the M.D.S.	
	8/5/18		General Louber had consultation with the A.D.M.S & C.R.E. 1st Divn. re proposed Gas Centre, and went on necessary alterations put in hand at once. Work in connection with improvements & structural alteration at the M.D.S. & A.D.S's will continue. Received information of an expected attack by the enemy. All necessary precautions taken ie, extra bearers sent up to the various posts & reserve personnel at H.Q. given the order to stand by.	Attached is plan of Gas Centre & scheme
	9/5/18		Visited front area to ensure that all arrangements for the reception & evacuation of wounded were in good order. Opened the Gas Centre at the M.D.S., got the treatment in the early stages of gas cases. One bearer sub division from 7 F.A. reported for duty with the Reserve Brigade, to be sent forward on receiving word from the A.D.M.S. All heavy equipment sent to Grand Servins (7t F.A.)	
	10/5/18		Situation for the last 24 hours normal. Still standing to.	

WAR DIARY or **INTELLIGENCE SUMMARY**

Army Form C. 2118

Sheet No. 2

B Field Ambulance May 1918

Place	Date	Hour	Summary of Events and Information	Remarks and references to Appendices
FOSSE 10	11/5/18		Situation normal. Bath working to.	
	12/5/18		Lt. Rogers of Mustard had previously admitted. Number of our bearers relieved by 7 F.A. Standing by "Leaders" relieved.	
	14/5/18		Situation normal. Visited front area to arrange re distribution of posts in the left centre scheme of evacuation. Had but contributed for the Evacuation & purification of gas cases.	
	15/5/18 to 18/5/18		General Routine. Situation normal. Work on improvement still continued. 21 cases of gas (shell) admitted on 17th inst.	
	19/5/18		Brig. 1st Army inspected M.D.S., Gas Centre & personnel.	
	20/5/18		General Routine. Bearers from 7th F.A. withdrawn from the front area, leaving only bearers of this unit to do the line work.	
	21/5/18		All Ambulance posts inspected by XVIII Corps D.S.M.T.O. on 24th inst.	
	22/5/18			
	25/5/18 to 28/5/18		General Routine. Nothing of importance to note.	
	29/5/18			
	30/5/18		Back area shelled hourly heavily by enemy artillery. Number of severely wounded admitted. Nothing further to note.	
	31/5/18			

Scheme of Evacuation. Front Area

R.A.P. (Tosh Keep)

A.D.S.
Fort Glatz.
{ 1. M.O.
1. Sgt.
1. Barber Cpl.
1. Reserve Cpl.
1. Clerk
1. Clerk Cpl. Orderly
4 Nursing Ordn.
10. G. Duty.

Ranic Post (St. Patricks)
{ 1. Lcpl.
5 men

Ranic Post Junction
{ 1. Cpl.
8 Men.

R.A.P.
Lens.
4 Men.

Ranic Post. Maroc
{ 1 Cpl.
4 Men.

A.D.S. (Cité St. Pierre)
{ 2. M.O.
1. Nursing Sgt
1. Reserve Sgt
4. N.O.
1. Cook
1. Clerk
20 G. Duty.

(Fosse 11)

(3 F.A. H.Q.)
M.D.S.
Fosse 10.

Diagrammatical Plan. Gas Centre.— 73 Fd. Ambce.

Evacuation of Cases other than Mustard.

FODEN LORRY

Tank of Bicarb. Sol. for bathing of clothes before Foden.

→ Lime Sol. for boots

Clothes lines

A = Treatment Tables

A = Venisection Table.

Ward for Cases awaiting evacuation.

Hip baths

Spray baths

Dressing & clothes Store room for Mustard Cases after bathing.

Water supply & Heating Apparatus.

Mustard Gas Cases

Gassed Cases other than mustard.

Treatment & Evacuation Ward for Mustard Gas Cases.

Classification Hut.

WINDOW.

Steps for Walking Cases

Shoes for Evacuation Stretcher Cases

✗ Door here only open when ward may be used for mustard Gas Cases (overflow).

WAR DIARY.

73rd. FIELD AMBULANCE

JUNE 1918.   VOLUME No. 34.

(ORIGINAL)

WAR DIARY
INTELLIGENCE SUMMARY

73 Field Ambulance
Sheet No. 1
Army Form C. 2118.
Map References Sheet 44A 1:44 & J
June 1918

Place	Date	Hour	Summary of Events and Information	Remarks and references to Appendices
FOSSE 10.	1/6/18		Owing to phosgene gas attack by the enemy, 73 gas cases were admitted, of whom 5 died in the Field Ambulance.	
	2/6/18 to 3/6/18		General Routine. A.D.M.S. went on leave — took over his duties. Nothing of importance to note.	
	4/6/18		Sent up a few extra bearers to A.D.S. 2nd Lieut. Geatz reported at 2002 Regt to help with possible casualties resulting from our raid.	
	5/6/18 to 9/6/18		General Routine. Nothing of importance to note.	
	10/6/18		About 20 gas cases passed through, chiefly caused by our own Chlorine Shift gas. D.D.M.S. Corps visited Main Dressing Station. All Ambulance cars at M.D.S. inspected by the M.T. Inspector, GHQ.	
	11/6/18		General Routine. A few cases of a new form of Influenza (Pyrexia) admitted. The symptoms found tho' a form of Influenza being new the area.	
	17/6/18 to 28/6/18		In spite of all precautions, the epidemic influenza spread very rapidly throughout the Division, and reached its maximum intensity on the 20th inst., when 465 cases passed through this unit. Special arrangements were made for supplying of antipyretics, the spraying of dugouts, and mouth washes and gargles for all contacts for all ranks actually dealing with the disease. The disease started on the right sector, and spread through the centre to the left Brigade. Over 60 Ranks of this unit were affected, the majority of whom were nursing orderlies, or	

73 Field Ambulance

Army Form C. 2118

WAR DIARY
or
~~INTELLIGENCE SUMMARY~~

(Erase heading not required.)

Instructions regarding War Diaries and Intelligence Summaries are contained in F.S. Regs., Part II. and the Staff Manual respectively. Title Pages will be prepared in manuscript.

Month and year: June 1918.

Sheet No.
Map references Sheets 44a 44b b.s.

Place	Date	Hour	Summary of Events and Information	Remarks and references to Appendices
FOSSE 10	17/6/18 to 19/6/18 (Contd.)		Reports who had been in direct contact with patients. During this period, 3800 cases of the epidemic passed through this unit, of whom 3366 were of the Division. For the collection & evacuation of sick, 3 motor lorries were sent by the Division, & 5 extra M.A. Cars were attached. These were from time to time supplemented by 10 cars from a neighbouring convoy. On the 19th inst., arrangements were made to turn the Gare Ouest No. 2 of the wards at the M.D.S. into a hospital for the epidemic, 140 cases being the maximum possible to retain. Three days later received the order for all cases to be evacuated to the Base, except those already convalescent. The majority of these cases were returned to duty after 7 days in hospital.	
	20/6/18 to 30/6/18		The epidemic is gradually dying out & comparatively few cases are passing through the unit. Most of the Rank ordered who were affected with the disease are now back but by no means well yet, only being fit for light duty. 630 cases through this period. There are no changes this month in the organization & administration of the front area, beyond continued improvements in the sanitary arrangements at the A.D.S.S. Nothing else of importance to note.	

7.7.18

[signature]
Lieut. Col. R.A.M.C.
O/C 73 Field Ambulance

140/3131.

No. 737. a.

73 FIELD AMBULANCE.

WAR DIARY — JULY 1918.

(ORIGINAL COPY)

VOLUME NO. 35.

Sheet 1.

Army Form C. 2118.

1/3 Field Ambulance

WAR DIARY
or
INTELLIGENCE SUMMARY
(Erase heading not required.)

Instructions regarding War Diaries and Intelligence Summaries are contained in F.S. Regs., Part II. and the Staff Manual respectively. Title Pages will be prepared in manuscript.

July 1918

Map references Sketch 44 a. 44 f.

V.L 35

Place	Date	Hour	Summary of Events and Information	Remarks and references to Appendices
FOSSE 10	1/7/18 to 4/7/18		General routine. During this period there was a decline in the number of epidemic pyrexia cases - only isolated cases arriving at this Unit. On 1st & 2nd inst., about 40 cases of gas poisoning admitted, suffering from Blue & Yellow Cross Gas. 20 N.C.O.s & men from the Division instructed in Chiropody - after 48 hours instruction these were sent for completion to No.6. 74 F.A. General medical situation normal.	
	5/7/18 to 12/7/18		General routine. Medical situation normal and practically no cases of epidemic pyrexia arriving. During this period, the A.D.M.S. 2st Div. made frequent inspections of the A.D.S.s at CITÉ ST PIERRE & FORT GLATZ, & of the front area generally. Nothing further to note.	
	13/7/18		Received Medical arrangements for use in the event of active operations, and visited the front area to arrange for new system of evacuation to the A.D.S. at FOSSE 11.	
	14/7/18		Visited A.D.S. FOSSE 11, with A.D.M.S. 2st Div, and discussed the question of turning the A.D.S. into a W.W.C.P.	
	15/7/18		Medical Arrangements (active operations) for this unit drafted, & approved by A.D.M.S. 2st Div. Medical situation normal, & the epidemic pyrexia has now died out in the Division.	Copy attached
	16/7/18		General routine. Arrangements put in hand at once for structural alterations &c, at FOSSE 11. The G.O.C. 2st Div., and D.D.M.S. VIII Corps visited the front area.	

Army Form C.2118.

73rd Field Ambulance Sheet 2.

WAR DIARY
or
INTELLIGENCE SUMMARY
(Erase heading not required.)

Instructions regarding War Diaries and Intelligence Summaries are contained in F. S. Regs., Part II. and the Staff Manual respectively. Title Pages will be prepared in manuscript.

Army Form C.2118.

Map references. Sheet 44 a { 44 b }

July 19/18

Place	Date	Hour	Summary of Events and Information	Remarks and references to Appendices
FOSSE 10.	17/7/18 to 22/7/18		General routine. Took over A.D.S. at FOSSE 11 from 72nd F. Amb. on 17.7.18, and began alterations after consultation with the A.D.M.S. and C.R.E. 24th Division. Medical situation normal. Nothing further of importance to note. J.W.Wynnington. Acting Lt. Col. R. Amb. O.C. 73rd Field Ambce.	
	23/7/18		Lt. Col. Cunningham, D.S.O., proceeded on leave to England, and Major Austin, M.C. assumed command of the unit.	
	24/7/18 to 31/7/18		General routine. Medical situation normal. On the 75th inst., 5 Officers & 8 O.R. from the 78th (U.S.A.) Divn. reported for instruction in the work of the forward area, etc. This party rejoined their unit on 30/7/18. On the 26th inst., party of men from various units of the Division reported for instruction in Sanitation — these handed over to O.C. No. 4. San. Section action. Reception to W. Col. at FOSSE 11 still proceeding. During the month the personnel were instructed in the application of Thomas's Splint. Nothing further of importance to note. Gus.Austin. Major R.Amb. a/OC 73 Field Ambulance	

73rd FIELD AMBULANCE.

In continuation of A.D.M.S. 24th Division, Medical Arrangements.

In the event of active operations :-

1. On receipt of message "Man Battle Stations" (Map 2), the M.Os. Nursing, Clerical and Cooking Staffs at A.D.Ss.- FORT GLATZ and ST.PIERRE will immediately withdraw to FOSSE 11.

    The N.C.O.s i/c Bearers, and bearers will remain until further orders from the Officer i/c A.D.S. FOSSE 11.

    The car or cars at LOOS and MAROC will report to Officer i/c A.D.S. FOSSE 11.

2. The abovementioned withdrawal parties will take with them as far as circumstances permit all F.A. equipment with the exception of a limited amount of dressings, stretchers and blankets for the R.M.O. taking over, and cooking utensils for the Bearer party left behind. Also all Red Cross Stores and remaining stretchers and blankets.

    At present there are at FORT GLATZ - Stretchers 30
    Blankets 51
    ST.PIERRE - Stretchers 20
    Blankets. 75

3. Major BRISCO, M.C. whether he is at H.Q. or A.D.S. at the time of warning, will immediately proceed to FOSSE 11 and take over charge of the A.D.S., Walking Wounded Post, and evacuations of front area.

    He will have under him three other Medical Officers, i.e. the Bearer Officers of 72 and 74 F.As. respectively, and one of the M.Os. from the evacuated A.D.Ss.

    In the event of his being at H.Q. at the time of withdrawal, he will detail one of the M.Os from the evacuated A.D.Ss. to report to the Main Dressing Station.

    Should any hitch occur in the evacuation, he will at his own discretion either detail one of the M.Os. under him to investigate the causes, or else investigate himself, leaving one of the other M.Os. temporarily in charge of the A.D.S.

4. Should Major RUDKIN, M.C. be one of the M.Os. at the A.D.Ss at time of warning, he will be the M.O. to report from the evacuated A.D.S. to the Main Dressing Station for general duty.

    In the event of the O.C. having to go to A.D.S. or R.A.Ps. he will immediately assume control of the M.D.S. and Gas Centre.

5. The Staff. Sergt. at A.D.S. FORT GLATZ will take over the duties of Senior N.C.O. at A.D.S. and W.W.Post, FOSSE 11.

    The Dispensing Sergt. at ST.PIERRE will take over the duties of Dressing Room Sergeant at FOSSE 11.

    As mentioned in para. 1, the Bearer Sergeants at FORT GLATZ and ST.PIERRE will remain there until they receive further orders from Major BRISCO.

6. On arrival of the Bearer Sections of 72 and 74 F.As. Major BRISCO will detail the necessary number for the Right and Centre Brigades, and on their taking over, will withdraw the bearers of 73 F.A. to FOSSE 11.

    The Bearers of the three F.As. at FOSSE 11 will act as loaders and general duty orderlies, and be available as reserves for any of the three Brigade fronts, and reliefs, at the discretion of the Officer in charge.

7. Should the Nursing, Clerical and Cooking staffs from A.D.Ss. FORT GLATZ and ST.PIERRE prove to be insufficient to work the combined A.D.S. and W.W.Post at FOSSE 11, the necessary reinforcements will be demanded from the Main Dressing Station.

8. Two runners will be detailed for each Brigade from the Bearer Section of the affiliated F.A.

9. The M.D.S. should be informed as soon as possible of any change in the dispositions which the Officer in charge of Advanced Area finds necessary to make.

10. MAROC Post will be taken over by the M.O. of the 12th Bn. Sherwood Foresters as a R.A.P., and the personnel there will be attached to him for the evacuation of his cases to FOSSE 11.

11. Evacuation from LOOS will be as far as possible by the trolley line direct to A.D.S. FOSSE 11. Otherwise by NORTH STREET TRENCH where relays will be arranged for stretcher cases to MAROC Post and thence to FOSSE 11.

Signature
Major R.A.M.C.
for Lieut.Col. R.A.M.C.
O.C. 73rd Field Ambulance.

73 FIELD AMBULANCE

WAR DIARY . AUGUST 1918

ORIGINAL COPY

VOLUME NO. 36.

7 Field Ambulance

Sheet 1.

WAR DIARY or INTELLIGENCE SUMMARY

Army Form C. 2118

August 1918

Map references: Sketch { LENS 11. 44 A / 44 B }

Place	Date	Hour	Summary of Events and Information	Remarks and references to Appendices
FOSSE 10 (SAINS)	1.8.18 2.8.18	—	General routine. Medical situation normal. Orders drafted for proposed "Set Down".	Copy attached
	3/8/18		"Set Down" & "Set Action" carried out on night of 3rd inst. Details as follows:—	
			M.D.S. O/C Set Down received 8.35 pm. Major Enrico M.C. & Heavy and Lgt. Back left for Fosse XI at 8.53 pm.	
			(2) Set Station received at 9.0 pm.	
			(a) 3 Sunbeams loaded with stores left for Fosse XI at 9.5 pm, 9.7 pm, & 9.11 pm respectively.	
			(b) Message despatched to Central Light Railway Control asking for train to be sent to Fosse XI at 9.5 pm.	
			(c) Telephone message received from Corps Tramway Office at 10.25 pm saying that a train was ready in the siding at PTX NOULETTE, & that he could always supply a train at one hours notice. Train not set up. Wire instructions from A.D.M.S. 24th Division.	
			(d) Beaney but Division home from Set Down arrived at M.D.S. at 11 pm.	
			(e) General remarks. The whole scheme appeared to work quite smoothly under the conditions existing at the time. Car drivers reported that the new road to Fosse XI was very rough and difficult to negotiate at night. (FOSSE XI)	

Army Form C. 2118

3 Field Ambulance   Sheet 2
WAR DIARY
or
INTELLIGENCE SUMMARY
(Erase heading not required.)

Instructions regarding War Diaries and Intelligence Summaries are contained in F.S. Regs., Part II August 1918 and the Staff Manual respectively. Title Pages will be prepared in manuscript.

Map references Sheet 11 {44 A 44 B}

Place	Date	Hour	Summary of Events and Information	Remarks and references to Appendices
FOSSE 10 (SAINS)	3/8/18		FOSSE XI (a) Major Brice, M.O. arrived at Fosse XI at 9.10 A.m. (b) All stores from M.D.S. arrived by 9.30 am (c) Last from A.D.S. Fort Glatz arrived at 10 p.m. with equipment & stores. (d) Nursing staff from Fort Glatz arrived 10.5 A.m. (e) Heart Sub division from 12 F.A. arrived 10.5 A.m. (f) Bearer Sub R.D.S. Lille St. Pierre arrived with Stores 10.40 p.m. (g) Personnel from Lille St. Pierre arrived 10.50 A.m. General remarks. The transference from the A.D.S's was carried out very successfully.	
	4/8/18 to 8/8/18		General Routine. Medical situation normal. Nothing further of importance to note.	
	9/8/18		Lce Cunningham, D.S.O. returned from leave	
	11/8/18		Bombing of Fosse 10 by enemy aeroplanes from 10 pm to 11 A.m. 42 cases admitted of whom 13 were civilians. All patients carried into cellars under Boys School, where a temporary dressing station was formed.	
	17/8/18		Orders rec'd to take over M.C.P at Fosse XI.	

Geo Rollin
Major Camb.
O/C 3 Field Ambulance
England.

Army Form C. 2118.

WAR DIARY or INTELLIGENCE SUMMARY

3/3 Field Ambulance. Sheet 3.

Instructions regarding War Diaries and Intelligence Summaries are contained in F. S. Regs., Part II. and the Staff Manual respectively. Title Pages August 1918 will be prepared in manuscript.

Map references Sheet 36 NW 11. 44 A. 44 B.

(Erase heading not required.)

Place	Date	Hour	Summary of Events and Information	Remarks and references to Appendices
FOSSE 10 (Sains)	13/8/18		Holding Party sent to N.W.C. at Fosse VI.	
	14/8/18 15/8/18		General Routine.	
	16/8/18		D.M.S. 1st Army visited M.D.S. and front area. Orders rec'd to take over D.R.S. from 3rd Fd. Amb. on 21.8.18.	
GRAND SERVINS	18/8/18 to 21/8/18		Arrangements made to relieve 1st Fd. Amb. Relief sent up in parties of about 20 at a time. Relief completed by 3pm. 21.8.18. 228 patients taken over.	
	22/8/18		General Routine. Work on improvements to camp commenced.	
	26/8/18		G.O.C. VIII Corps visits D.R.S.	
	27/8/18		General Routine. Medical situation normal. Nothing of importance to note. 189 patients returned to duty during month.	
	28/8/18 to 31/8/18			

J.H. Cunningham
Capt. A.A.M.C.
O.C. 3/3 Field Amb.

73rd FIELD AMBULANCE.

1. A test "Prepare for Action" and a test "Man Battle Stations" will be carried out shortly.
   The O.i/c A.D.Ss. ST.PIERRE and FORT GLATZ will receive the commands "Test Action" and "Test Stations" from the Brigades in whose section they are situated.

2. Both A.D.Ss. will continue to function as such throughout the test and in consequence the following alteration in procedure to that detailed in the "Man Battle Positions" orders already issued will be carried out.

3. On receipt of command "Test Action" all equipment and stores at A.D.Ss. FORT GLATZ and ST.PIERRE will be packed up and the personnel as detailed in the previous order will be prepared to move.

4. On command "Test Stations" the Officer i/c A.D.S. will detail the N.C.O. i/c, the Clerical and Cooking staffs, and half the Nursing Staff to proceed via the Light Railway track to FOSSE XI. He will send as much equipment and stores as possible by car to FOSSE XI accompanied by a detailed list.
   The Officer i/c A.D.S. ST.PIERRE will act in the same way except that the N.C.O. i/c Dressing Room will remain at the A.D.S.

5. The O.i/c A.D.S. FOSSE XI will ask the Central Control Post AIX NOULETTE for a train to be sent up.

6. After inspections personnel will return to their normal dispositions under orders from the A.D.M.S.

7. An accurate time record of every detail of the test will be kept by all officers concerned and a full report stating any difficulties, suggestions, etc will be sent to H.Q. F.A. as soon as possible after completion of test.

Confidential

73rd Field Ambulance

WAR DIARY
(ORIGINAL)

FOR THE MONTH OF

SEPTEMBER 1918.

Volume N° 37.

Army Form C. 2118.

73rd Field Ambulance.

WAR DIARY
or
INTELLIGENCE SUMMARY.
(Erase heading not required.)

Map Sheet 44B
September 1918.

Instructions regarding War Diaries and Intelligence Summaries are contained in F. S. Regs., Part II. and the Staff Manual respectively. Title pages will be prepared in manuscript.

Place	Date	Hour	Summary of Events and Information	Remarks and references to Appendices
	1.9.18 to 6.9.18		General routine. Medical situation normal. Inspections made on Water Carts, general sanitation and water bottles. Unit sports held. Weather showery and cold.	
	7.9.18 to 8.9.18		General routine. Nothing of importance to note. Medical situation still normal. Weather very wet during this period. Gas drill carried out daily.	
	9.9.18 to 29.9.18			
	30.9.18		Relieved by 2/3 Home Counties Field Ambulance. Moved to HERSIN arriving at 3.30pm. Orders received to entrain early next morning for MONDICOURT area. Transport proceeded by road to new area.	

J.M. Munnington
Lt Col RAMC
O.C. 73rd Field Ambulance

Army Form W.3091.

Cover for Documents.

Nature of Enclosures.

N/3. Field Ambulance

for month of Oct. 1918

Notes, or Letters written.

WAR DIARY

733 FIELD AMBULANCE

OCTOBER 1918   VOL. 38

(DUPLICATE COPY)

WAR DIARY or INTELLIGENCE SUMMARY

Army Form C. 2118

7th Field Ambulance October 1918

Maps Reference: LENS 11 57 D 57 C 57 A

Place	Date	Hour	Summary of Events and Information	Remarks and references to Appendices
HERSIN	1.10.18		Unit left pre-short entrained at HERSIN (LENS 11) at 09.15 hrs, and detrained at MONDICOURT (Sheet 57D); from thence marched to MILLY (A.1.6.9.4.) arriving about 18.00 hrs. Transport arrived at 16.00 hrs, having travelled by road. All men billeted in barns.	
MILLY	2.10.18 to 4.10.18		Arrangements made for erection of bayde Sect. Training for open warfare carried out — tent pitching, collection of wounded &c.	
— "—	5.10.18		Unit arrived by road to forward area, leaving MILLY at 0800 hrs.	
— "—	6.10.18		Enemy orders for personnel received. Unit left MILLY at 13.15 hrs & marched to MONDICOURT. Entrained at 16.30 hrs & arrived at HAVRINCOURT about midnight. From there marched to	
HAVRINCOURT	7.10.18		E.22.b.7.0 (Sheet 57C) arriving about 03.00 hrs, 7.10.18. Personnel accommodated in bivouacs. Tents & cookers with transport arrived 2 miles N. rear. Weather fine but cold. Received orders to move further forward. Marched at 15.00 hrs to L.2.a.0.0. arriving about 16.30. Reconnoit out & division in readiness for the morning attack.	

7th Field Ambulance
October 1918   Sheet 2.

WAR DIARY or INTELLIGENCE SUMMARY

Army Form C. 2118

Place	Date	Hour	Summary of Events and Information	Remarks and references to Appendices
NOYELLES	8.10.18		Heavy enemy shelling in the back area. 5 men of the unit being wounded. Orders received to take over A.D.S. NOYELLES CHATEAU (L.11.6 Central) and all fools from advances of 63rd Division. Relief completed by 2200 hrs. Stretcher bearer sub-divisions now with various battalions of the Brigade.	
–	9.10.18		Infantry attacked 0530 hrs. Very few of our men, but a good number of German prisoners through the A.D.S. during the day. Gain of ground a few further hundred at short notice. Opened A.D.S. NOYELLES at 0600 hrs, until transport so proceeded to G.16.d.7.4. (near Rumilly) & there Divisional instructions. At 0900 hrs	
–	10.10.18		received word to came forward & reopened an A.D.S. Action was taken immediately and an A.D.S. formed at the Sugar Factory at A.8.d.8.8. (Sheet 57 B) at 1130 hrs. There in the line relieved by reserve troops during the day.	
108 & 8.8 (57 B)	11.10.18		Enemy again attacked in the morning - about 600 cases passed through the A.D.S. during the day. Weather now unsettled.	

Army Form C. 2118.

... 73 Field Ambulance   Sheet 3.

WAR DIARY
or
INTELLIGENCE SUMMARY

(Erase heading not required.)

Instructions regarding War Diaries and Intelligence Summaries are contained in F. S. Regs., Part II. October 1918 and the Staff Manual respectively. Title Pages will be prepared in manuscript.

Place	Date	Hour	Summary of Events and Information	Remarks and references to Appendices
68 t. 8. 9 (17A)	9.10.18		Few wounded now passing through. A.D.S. not closed.	a 74 F.A.
	12.10.18		Faded though, & formed an A.D.S. further forward. Orders received to pack & await further instructions.	
	14.10.18			
RIEUX	15.10.18		Advance party proceeded to RIEUX (57A) at 09.30 hours. Remainder of unit left at 10.30 & reached RIEUX about 12.00 hrs.	
	16.10.18		1 O. & 14 O.R.s sent up with Bedfords Regt.	
CAMBRAI	17.10.18		Relieved by 17th Bn.Div. & proceeded to outskirts of CAMBRAI. Bivouaced at A.I.Sd. 2.8 (Sheet 57A)	
	18.10.18		Moved to billets at A.20.a.0.7.	
	19.10.18 20.10.18		Nothing of importance to note. Orders received having orders to move to Quiévy at 17.h. Bn. (20.10.18)	
HAUSSY	26.10.18		Marched in rear of Brigade to HAUSSY (57A) and arrived at 15.30 hrs.	
	27.10.18 to 30.10.18		Nothing of importance to note. Everything nearly the same. A.D.S. at above nature.	
	31.10.18		Service division took part in tactical manoeuvre by the 7.I.D. Nothing further to note.	

J.B. Mumming Lt.
Lieut. R.C. R.A.M.C.
O.C. 73 Field Ambulance

73rd. FIELD AMBULANCE.

WAR DIARY.

November 1918.   Original Copy.

Volume No. 39

Army Form C. 2118.

73rd Field Ambulance.

WAR DIARY
INTELLIGENCE SUMMARY
(Erase heading not required.)

Nov. 1918

Place	Date	Hour	Summary of Events and Information	Remarks and references to Appendices
HAUSSY	1.11.18		Received orders to proceed to Bermerain at 1640 hrs on 2.11.18. Bearer sub-division attached to the 3 Regiments of 73 I.B.	Sheet 51A
	2.11.18		Advance parties sent to school at Bermerain at 0800 hrs. These opened an A.D.S. at approx. Q22.c.0.9. Remainder of the ambulance with transport, left Haussy 1640 hrs, and reached Bermerain about 1930 hrs. All posts in the forward area taken over from the 6th Divn. Reconnoitred advanced area for site for an advanced A.D.S. The brewery at Sepmeries (approx. Q.6.b.8.6.) found to be suitable, and arrangements made to occupy it. [crossed out] Hostile artillery fairly active during the night in the back area.	
BERMERAIN	3.11.18		Orders re coming operations received. A clearing party sent to Q.6.b.8.6, to be ready at Zero hour to open an A.D.S. Advance party to work the A.D.S. proceeded about 1700 hrs. Very few cases received during the night.	
SEPMERIES	4.11.18		Casualties after the attack at 0530 hrs began to arrive about 0700 hrs. Proceeded at 1000 hrs to Villers Pol to find new site for A.D.S. at this hour, headquarters of unit ordered from Bermerain to Sepmeries. Advance party sent at 1400 hrs to open A.D.S. at Villers Pol. (134.d.5.7.) Altogether about 360 cases received during the day – 250 at Sepmeries & the remainder at Villers Pol.	
VILLERS POL				

73 Field Ambulance.   Sheet No. 2

Army Form C. 2118

Nov. 1918.

WAR DIARY
or
INTELLIGENCE SUMMARY
(Erase heading not required.)

Place	Date	Hour	Summary of Events and Information	Remarks and references to Appendices
VILLERS POL	5.11.18		Headquarters unit reached Villers Pol about 0300 hrs. A.D.S. that at 0630 hrs. at 7th F.A. had proceeded to WARGNIES le GRAND. Had opened an A.D.S. there. Orders received to stand by & be ready to proceed to an advanced post at a moments notice.	
ST WAAST	7.11.18		Received orders to form an A.D.S. at ST WAAST at further forward if possible. Proceeded to do so & went & opened A.D.S. at 1700 hrs. Not wet. Many cases received. Working party sent to BAVAY filled the college. As this time BAVAY was though[t] the objective for an A.D.S. Advance party opened A.D.S. at BAVAY (T.L. F.0.6) at 1100 hrs.	
BAVAY	8.11.18		About 50 cases received. Weather wet.	
	9.11.18 10.11.18 11.11.18		Nothing to note of importance up to cessation of hostilities.	
WARGNIES	16.11.18 17.11.18		Moved with Brigade Group to WARGNIES LE GRAND.	
ROUVIGNIES	18.11.18		March onwards to Rouvignies	
AUBERCHICOURT	19.11.18		"Auberchicourt". Units now under administration of VIII Corps (First Army).	
	20.11.18 21.11.18		Provided with Brigade Group to Renegies came under administration of I Corps.	
	22.11.18		Marched to Mouchin (Sheet 44. F.28 a. 3.8)	
	23.11.18 30.11.18		Light training, fatigues &c. Football &c. in the afternoon.	

J.B. Summerson
Lieut. Col. R.A.M.C.
O.C. 73 Field Ambulance

Confidential

73rd Field Ambulance

War Diary

for the month of

December, 1918.

Army Form C. 2118

73rd Field Ambulance

WAR DIARY
or
INTELLIGENCE SUMMARY

(Erase heading not required.)

Map Reference Sheet No. 37

Instructions regarding War Diaries and Intelligence Summaries are contained in F.S. Regs., Part II. and the Staff Manual respectively. Title Pages will be prepared in manuscript.

December, 1918

Place	Date	Hour	Summary of Events and Information	Remarks and references to Appendices
Field	1-12-18 to 6-12-18		Nothing unknown to note.	
	7-12-18		1 Officer & 2 OR's sent to 17 mgo inspection on ROUBAIX – TOURNAI road. One tent Sub division sent to No 51 C.C.S. TOURNAI for temporary duty.	
	8-12-18 to 17-12-18		Light training, whole revived, football etc in afternoon.	
	18-12-18		Moved to FLORENT. Wigany & personnel billeted in Monastery.	
	19-12-18 to 24-12-18		Nothing of importance. Light training etc	
	25-12-18		Christmas Day. Church Service. Dinners arranged for personnel, followed by concert.	
	26-12-18 to 30-12-18		Usual training etc	
	31-12-18		Twenty OR's proceeded to U.K. during the month for release on Coalminers.	

Leo Prince
Major. R.A.M.C.
40.6 73 Field Ambulance

24 DIV

BOX 1952

Confidential

73rd Field Ambulance. R.A.M.C

War Diary
for the month of January. 1919.

Army Form C. 2118.

WAR DIARY
or
INTELLIGENCE SUMMARY

73rd Field Ambulance

January 1919.

(Erase heading not required.)

Place	Date	Hour	Summary of Events and Information	Remarks and references to Appendices
Field	1-1-19 to 31-1-19		Nothing of importance to note. Usual training & recreation. Educational Classes held daily. 19 O.Rs proceeded to U.K during the month for release.	

John Cunningham
Lieut Col E. Rampe
O.C. 73rd Field Ambulance

Confidential

73rd Field Ambulance
War Diary for month of
February, 1919.

Army Form C. 2118.

73rd Field Ambulance.

WAR DIARY
or
INTELLIGENCE SUMMARY

(Erase heading not required.)

February 1919.

Instructions regarding War Diaries and Intelligence Summaries are contained in F. S. Regs., Part II. and the Staff Manual respectively. Title Pages will be prepared in manuscript.

Place	Date	Hour	Summary of Events and Information	Remarks and references to Appendices
Seed.	1.2.19 to 28.2.19.		Nothing of importance to note. Usual training & recreation. Educational classes held daily. 30 O.R's proceeded to U.K. during the month for release. 1 Officer	

Farrell
Major R.A.M.C
O.C. 73rd Field Ambulance.

Confidential

73rd Field Ambulance
War Diary for the month of
March. 1919.

Army Form C. 2118.

WAR DIARY
or
INTELLIGENCE SUMMARY

73rd Field Ambulance

(Erase heading not required.)

Instructions regarding War Diaries and Intelligence Summaries are contained in F. S. Regs., Part II. and the Staff Manual respectively. Title Pages will be prepared in manuscript.

March 1919.   Sheet 37   1/40,000

Place	Date	Hour	Summary of Events and Information	Remarks and references to Appendices
TAINTIGNIES (BELGIUM)	1-3-19 to 31-3-19		All surplus vehicles handed into D.A.D.S.T. Remainder of transport with the exception of 1 limber parked at 24th Div Vehicle Park. BAISIEUX (Div Cadre Concentration Area). All animals with the exception of 1 Tyler Draught & 1 Heavy Draught sent away. Unit gradually reduced to Cadre strength. The 13 O.R's retainable for Army (No exceptions despatched) as follows:- Six sent to 29th Division June " - No. 2 C.C.S. Two " - D.G.M.S. Offices 51 O.R's proceeded to U.K. during the month for release.	

G W Ruell
Major RAMC
OC 73 Field Ambulance

Confidential

73rd Field Ambulance
War Diary
for the month of
April, 1919.

Army Form C. 2118.

WAR DIARY
or
INTELLIGENCE SUMMARY

73rd Field Ambulance

(Erase heading not required.)

Map Reference: Sheet 37.   April, 1919.

Instructions regarding War Diaries and Intelligence Summaries are contained in F. S. Regs., Part II. and the Staff Manual respectively. Title Pages will be prepared in manuscript.

Place	Date	Hour	Summary of Events and Information	Remarks and references to Appendices
Field	1-6		Nothing of importance to note.	
	7/4/19		Left FLORENT and marched to ANSTAING (FRANCE) Sheet 37. M.26.t.3.8 (Concentration Area). Personnel billeted in a Chateau.	
	8.4.19 to 30.4.19		Weather cold & wet. Nominals remaining with unit are now, the last two having been sent away on 10.4.19 — 1 Officer & 1 O.R. proceeded to U.K. during the month for release. 6 O.Rs R.A.M.C. and 4 O.Rs R.A.S.C. (H.T.) also were available owing to demobilization. Very few sick admitted during the month.	

[Signature] Surrell
Major R.A.M.C.
M.O.C. 73rd Field Ambulance

www.ingramcontent.com/pod-product-compliance
Lightning Source LLC
Chambersburg PA
CBHW080851230426
43662CB00013B/2077